The Land of the Dead Is Open for Business

The Land of the Dead Is Open for Business

Jacob Strautmann

Four Way Books
Tribeca

For Valerie, Northanna, and Ernest Marlowe,
and in memory of Sean D. Reilly.

Library of Congress Cataloging-in-Publication Data

Names: Strautmann, Jacob, author.
Title: The land of the dead is open for business / Jacob Strautmann.
Description: New York : Four Way Books, [2020]
Identifiers: LCCN 2019031739 | ISBN 9781945588464 (trade paperback)
Subjects: LCSH: West Virginia--Poetry. | Capitalism--Environmental
aspects--West Virginia--Poetry. | Capitalism--Social aspects--West
Virginia--Poetry. | Environmental degradation--West Virginia--Poetry. |
Offenses against the environment--West Virginia--Poetry. |
Nature--Effect of human beings on--West Virginia--Poetry.
Classification: LCC PS3619.T74345 A6 2020 | DDC 811/.6--dc23
LC record available at https://lccn.loc.gov/2019031739

This book is manufactured in the United States of America and printed on
acid-free paper.

Four Way Books is a not-for-profit literary press. We are grateful for the assistance
we receive from individual donors, public arts agencies, and private foundations.

This publication is made possible with public funds from the
New York State Council on the Arts, a state agency.

We are a proud member of the Community of Literary Magazines and Presses.

Contents

The Boy and the Rafter

This was the summer after the winter
the coal stoves of our neighbors upwind
dropped flocks of commas on the parable of snow.
Noon crickets slept. The wind abandoned
August and our trailer—that's when voices
lulled me back, pressed my face to split-glass
windows cranked wide to see whom I heard,
what had gathered in our new foundation
still cut mud-open. Birds lumbered through
discovering their place amongst themselves,
clumps of rank and retinue, dear purple
draping their feathered congress. How suddenly
silent they were, bowing and sidling like men
unused to looking at each other. What I thought
took on the silver tinge of dream. I doubted
even then what I knew I could never forget,
and I have forgotten everything they said,
their bulbous shifting and speckled necks
where a cacophony of light opened
to catch the truth, like amethysts I remember
spinning on a necklace of leaving what can
no longer be, and never like they knew it.

Death of a Young Girl in the Town of Cameron, West Virginia

Years later, a tree falls
from the hillside of her cemetery
across route two-fifty's hairpin turn
crushing a moving car, the man inside.

What's Left

. . . .*It seems your mother is not your mother,*
You are not you, home is an alien land.
—*Pasternak*

Every earring, every hole punched penny,
and feathers blowing from the open coop
baked in a half-mask of light sharp as seeds.
Here was another language: a red circle, rusted
square wrote *fallow*; a zipper of bones
made *bird*, her little faces inside out,
like white cornhusks blistering our farm
the ridge-cap healed under. Another run,

a turn, there was nothing to forgive,
precambrian death magnificently still
but for the moon, that living pockmark,
stitching it all back, pulling bare the threaded night.
The curtain shook, the wind rising.
When I said *parent*, I meant topography.

Mother's Day

Dig for potatoes, brush the earth from their faces.
Under the tap, scrub them with wool, like smoke,
as the television scrolls with names, white letters
on a blue background. Start the water to boil,
because you forgot to start it before. The dull
propane hisses. The peeler chases your thumb
around each one, over the sink, morning's one dish.
A hand with a knife works them into halves,
then quarters of themselves, then nothing.
When you push them from the cutting board,
scald your arm, wince, and sweep the rest
with the knife's edge. This is necessary;
it isn't the only thing left with which to fill
your day, but nearly. It's nearly the only thing.

The Coconut

Sunday light, white formica table,
coconut spinning in the middle—
my cousin's gift from a volcanic
slope. My hand's a child's—
fork, flathead, ballpeen hammer.
Grandma wields a paring knife,
holds me from the blade.

Sun sweeps a strip of amber shadow
across the room, a fly trap's measure
of innocence, flour drifting
across the counter's desert islands.
Chicken in the skillet sizzles.
The coconut holds us in circumference,
in an uncrackable wholeness.

Down the hall, Pap clears his lung,
curtains drawn, the living room dark.
In the woodstove, a fire banks
too high for April. He knows (I know)
the fruit, the flesh and heaven of it;
around him linoleum lifts yellow
compositions of glue,

and out his dim window, a mud-dauber's
long legs revise her scrolls in a rib
of aluminum siding, her backlit
image patterned on lace grows,
recedes, grows. Grandma lifts
the open-fisted coconut, as if to say,
"hold it to your mouth like a man."

The Volunteers

The farmhouse leans in light
the landscape holds exquisitely.
In a crescent men watch the scorch-
wind, eyes as dry as gravel spades.

Clapboards curl. The frame pops
its locks and birds abandon; out
the cellar door mice twist and bolt.
A black tree sings from the center

of total loss. Years, years pass.
The landlords rent a dozer
their nephew throttles to cover
the ditch: a piano's charred lip,

ivory teeth pressed to the clay,
mess of wire and flashing,
and skulls of marsh ducks coddled
in luxuriant fronds, rusted tub.

He buries the mason jars. A porcelain
cracks, spits frogs, collapses.
The dirt tamps, the diesel buckets
heave a last good turn.

Advice for a Mountain Laureate

Resist enough.
A buck-knife grips its butcher-song.
Be abeyant, sharp, hanging on a hook.

See kudzu thrive, reclaim
unemployment office parking lots.
And when an ambulance opens its doors
to the portal of a mine,
swallow more.

Open your big, garish heart,
that fiery steel furnace, men—some deaf,
some dead—banked day and night for years.

Leave us by going in.

Swamp Maple

for my sister

Laundry ripped down by the armful
at full run flickers brightly on the ground;
sunflowers lean on propane tanks, and manes
of horses, combed straight at morning,
rise like Arabic script to a smaller sky
fenced in by the dune-rough clouds.
Acres, too, foreshorten in the glaze
of seventy years of sudden downpour.
Dandelions in rain dip like little men
we grew away from in our childhoods.
We were taller and cleaner then, with air
inside our clothes, the air that warns the hillside,
pushes before it the smell of a neighbor's woods—
birdnest-scatter, a clump of fur dancing on a post.

Goshorn Ridge Proposals

A flick of her tongue
Was wind crossing fence and swishing mares.
On contour maps of Cameron District,
Marshall County, W.Va., men
Ripple in isolation,
What's unlikely to be written well;
Their muscular turning away is
Sentiment caricatured,
Dry leaves drilled by rain until they break.

"Don't Do Me Like That"

The dirt road plummets off Sutton Hill where Viola's
bone-cattle hoof the crickside of 1979.

Grandmothers curdled in shacks chant *Hare
Hare Krishna*. They were young once, too.

We're taking bets. Sheriff's at the Black Flag
since Tuesday, and you'll never clear

the stink of mouse out of a Trans Am's vent.
Doesn't mean we can't dare you to pop

the clutch, crank your window, bellow
whatever the hell crass thing you need.

July dust thickens on the leaves. Everyone
is waiting for what will never come;

so go on, we need a good rip. Flip us the bird,
John-Boy. Gun it. Spit gravel. Get.

Elementary Monster

He tried to be good, less watchful. They stuck
blue ribbons to his sweaty shag rug cut toga.
Under the backboard, girls wore felts and pins;
his cannibal's painted skin, halloween gaze
circled back like the dog in his heart to their
thin, small fingers, twirling white stocking feet.
There was a black line between them, physical,
an idea racing out to touch the thing
it could disguise, disfigure, in the furnace
of colors, as all the others tore ripshit out
gymnasium doors and turned their hideous
faces, counting their blessings.

South Garden

Forgive our cultivated ugliness I won't, and even if we'd seen it through
a third growing, believe me, I'd be a mean toothless liar like Pappaw.
Flat rocks slick with garter snakes, squash we never planted, groundhogs
our dogs dragged to the till line. Corn, flowers, a cold unmoving eye.

Virginity could mean nothing there with possum, milksnake abloom in
    the ragweed,
and all the dead soul words I knew the square fence rusted around.
We kept his tiller for years wrapped in a yellow tarp. The shock of death
was his flag fraying under the pine. Daddy long-legs shuttled

some towards, some circling the meat of my finger. By then we'd ripped
    it out:
a place for my bike, for living things. He meant well. He meant nothing
    at all.
My mother lay beside him, unbuckling the degenerative vertebrae.
We kept death, and he kept us. She kept those years in a mason jar.

The Leap

Eighth grader,
older cousin,
clucks her tongue
and kicks
the soft flank lightly;
we jolt forward
faster than breath.
I'm crushed between
her grip on the horn,
hand on the reins,
as the black animal
finds air, whirligig
of mare, sky, ground
passes like integers read
in quick succession.
PVC balances
on the barrels where
my cousin looks back
as we canter downhill;
how should I know
I cause the thing I fear
the most? Legs gone rigid—.
The sudden smell
of morning I join

in falling through
the hickory leaves,
the miracle of landing
on our backs unharmed.
The taste of horse
sweat blocks the sight
of the double-wide filled
with aunts: Barbara and Joyce
and Linda and Linda,
their Slims, oblivious I
know the gravity of my body
in the gravity-bound day.

There's Someone at the Door

You flew up into yourself from the lower right hand corner of our photograph,
flew up, startled the nests that shook in our hair. Our faces downcast sobbed for you—
once for sorrow, once for the magpie on your shoulder, once for your white wisp and laugh.
You made dumb trees of us standing around, and the lake was calm, wide as the sky.

Flew up, startled the nests that shook in our hair. Our faces downcast sobbed for you,
leaning on the house inside us. We wanted to say something to your sons;
you made dumb trees of us standing around, and the lake was calm, wide as the sky.
This is our memory, a cloudbank passing quickly with shadows on the ground.

When we heard the wind at the gate, we wanted to say anything to your sons—
you flew up into yourself from the lower right hand corner of our photograph.
This is our memory, a cloudbank passing quickly with shadows on the ground,
once for sorrow, once for the magpie on your shoulder, once for your white wisp and laugh.

My Father's Father's Cadillac

The blue inherited Eldorado
Jacked up fourteen months
On blocks:

My father remembers his, as sure
As the crack in the manifold.
Motor turn over, won't turn over.

Here is our temple, when all the farmers
Leave their ticking utility vehicles,
Pre-fab shelters, and tiny crops

Of mostly hay and cribcorn and tractors
To visit a god wrapped in a tarp,
Hood wide. My father calls to his

Craftsman, ratcheting lower, his
Carhart-brown now submarine.
We stand a circle of acetylene silence.

Our lands around us dim, fence us in;
Mines hum and someone in the hollow
Keeps a rooster, where night falls quickly.

I lower the lantern past the engine block.
He's somewhere down there. I lower
It—like a question I could have asked.

Motor turn over, won't turn over.

Honey Locust

We crossed the ruts, tadpoles the flat rocks canted over,
a drainage ditch you called a *run* sunk against stone,
and, when you pressed my rainy fingers to your thigh,
white roots uncoiled at our backs. For fifteen minutes
I fell in love, and you, as cicadas wheezed on bark,
said, *listen for engines rifling past in coffins of dust.*
The men your stepdad hired to truss the slouching roof
and slam the doors of rented campers on the bend—,
their laughter rode my ear persistent as a truth
half-told, as you were tempted by the ridgelines, wild
clay-sulching culverts, the scent of hayricks after snow,
to tell it half, to show me something of the rest,
and for that—my not knowing you—you loved me, though
momentarily, as the hillside does the season.

Commencement Day, Banks of the Ohio

Splitting that stratum from the Ohio, we were a speck of white
harnessed to the mid-May-weighted skies.

Imagine they are waiting for us. You said, *us*, to test the dark
ribbon pulling us outward as Rte. 2 wed the mined-out hill

we rounded in your Subaru. White-knuckled, I imagined

loving the bridge of your lips pressing bobby pins
in the basement of a church, the bouquet gathered up,

as my heart slipped from its saddle of ribs beside the river,
a smokestack, a landscape cleft.

This could be my apology. Rising ahead, a kingbird

shakes his foil out on the turn, sister constellations open
like crocuses. Working men holler, whip up their caps, beckon

your fingers, your hand to my hand—white celebration.
I said nothing. Still can't. With long unmoving faces,

our families sit mother to mother watching the door for a sign.

Par Avion

Did you see the sky on the twenty-third
green and black over itself tumbling
like a nest of snakes opened in hard light?
Enclosed: the telescope, as promised.
Keep it dressed in its warm and red-lipped case.
Poems may follow. Yesterday I cleared
the well-house. The moving jaws of copperheads,
little heads lined up on a concrete floor,
laughing at the blood-spackled hoe,
at the whole miserable operetta,
reminded me of something Greek I read.
Chanting never brought anyone home.

Cold the Terrible Water

My grandfather loved Glenn Miller,
and when his music plays I see
the woman I would one day cut out,
who went with me to his graveside
the week after, who watched me arrange
the clippings and the silent trombones,
knew when to step over the mud-sinks,
take my hand, and kiss me, a bird call
lifting the dew-soaked evergreens,
the bell of our hidden faces. In the end,
everything is quiet, as these loves of ours
wage again for something more substantial
than the monument given them, a language
for the cupped places we hold them in.

She Longed to Be a Bird, Whitetail, Stray Dog

sliding out crooked in the birth night of summer,
screen door thrum, aluminum siding in the porchlight.
She pulls apart the barbed-wire fence. Torn tail

and mane brush her throat. She crouches into
the darkest pasture and dew-wet passages
downhill, for the pond below that a farmer

backhoed decades before. And further down
a run overspills with newborn crawdads
and the blacker than black shale on shale.

Her porchlight blazes and whimpers.
A solitary trunk as cold as a branch
shoved in mud shares the pondside.

She was her husband slipping for years
to different corners of the yard. She was
her children the ridgelines crossed through.

Their absence pools in the diesel track.
Gentle fingers gesture to the run,
and the blacker than black, and the thrill.

The Joyful Noise Choir, Wolf Run Presbyterian

They stand—most of the multitude—to sing,
farmers, wives of farmers, struck in the pews,
and when the end arrives and no one claps,
they know to sit back in the creaking place

they'd risen from. Like a dry knucklebone,
a John Deere throttles, pops, machine-guns past.
A cloud of grasshoppers spits across the panes
sagging in their peeling sleeves, and the rows

of stones in the yard settle deeper in.
He that hath ears to hear, let him hear!
that the diesel lifts a rusted mower, veers
cumbersome towards the west in the far field.

From where they sit they know a widow slows
her tractor, mops her brow, replaces her husband's
blaze orange cap and drops the blades again.
For most, no noise would cut the sermon out.

The Gift

From crickside tin camps where antennae rub leather
with the moonlight and car scrap nesting on the water's edge,
the hills circle back, a pack of tails and teeth. Listen
over Big Wheeling Creek—hills are blue with poverty.
Up deer paths, hear Krishna Ridge cabins whose leaves,
mattresses and Gîtâs spook the floor, where my uncle
found solace, scabies, a woman who gave herself
a holy name in the summer.

                  Scent of the run puddles
below a locust black sky shaking tambourines
against an aluminum bedroom wall for a boy possessed
by the sound of it, guarding the wet stump of it,
like quarry, like honey at the root of a black tongue.
Through every dark window it crawls, what my neighbor
Richard Fitzsimmons might have said, his knee
turned sideways by a cow: what I hear trembling
on his voice, his dear friend Joseph pinned forty years
under a tractor out Wolf's Run, desire as blue as the pines.

The Poet Arrives at the Former Site of the John Brown Trailer Park

I crossed the riverbed at Harpers Ferry
southwest for your ribs, Allegheny.
There's news.
Thursday, rapture-like, everyone moved on,
left even Charleston silent, grey,
legislators scraping down
the Kanawha on sandpapery skin.
Your camps and unincorporateds
closed their eyes, descended in
a blue tattoo of oxycontin.
Land-of-my-Mothers-but-not-of-my-Children,
of Appalachian Redevelopment Commissions,
now birds die here, and seeds
in summer hayfields molder. Sheep
birth limp two-headed things and some
that speak like men if they speak at all.
We grew up in a tin can shaking
in the wind, stayed as long as we could,
bargained the hill like the soul leaves
her body for a city full of people and work.
You could have noticed, could have called
us back, could have called Richmond,
Pittsburgh, Cincinnati, Baltimore,

but we cut your metal bonds,
vibrating hillsides, your flat acres
of not much value, not much music.

Fork Ridge Right-of-Way

A toyota-shaped slipstream
plucks the tines of dying maples
between the blacktop and the new
compressor plant. Their clumps of
clawed leaves wither, wait, copper
Hopewell spearmen, for the burn.
My mother at the wheel asks politely
why don't I move back.
You murderous, blessed, clinquant
compressor plant: You hypertrophic
tinman cathedral, perfected,
microchip perfected
child of the smokestacks west
on the river nosing stars: You forked
tongue of the hills, death
unmetaphorical and grieved,
bare-breasted and diademed:
our haute couture: most complete
poem! It's as if You allow us
to take the turn. It's as if You count
Your family complete. The fox
in the dead of the night
compromises coop and hutch,
coop and hutch, as new pipelines

cut a farm's hills square, and wages
blow through beautiful as
dirt hanging in the air,
how I hold Mom's hand in mine
before she steals away.

Mayor Betty's Cameron Crawdad Fest

Each spring they throw a Crawdad Fest
(the "f" in "fest"—pincers and a tail
painted red on a white sail
tacking from 2nd Best Dressed

to Lou's Taxidermy Studios
top floor "Observation Wing").
It was all the Mayor's thing
after her husband chose

the trucker's life, left her to raise
seven dull-eyed sons
seven years ago, the sons
she groomed, called her Grace,

(her private test) who through sheer will
she crowned the Crawdad King
six years running with sponsoring
businesses as far as Moundsville.

Her Administration took up the cause—
once, her in-law's grill in May—
to celebrate the Municipality,
revitalized as well as it ever was,

and possibly entice new funds
for the city building's leaky roof;
the 10% they raised was proof
it worked as well as raffling guns.

Ramp Hunting

Look for them on the northern slope
wrapped in spiderlings of shade
the locust spinneret on April,

broad leaves and purple stems
flourishing in pockets that two boys,
set free from chores, were sent collecting.

Girls' names, like horses' whips,
ghost wet shapes on the hillsides
half an hour in, and the ramps bulge

Kroger sacks; a cigarette
passes through
the ceremony made of breaking rules.

The oldest holds it in and counts,
grit and squint, lungs revving—
when echoes loud as railroad-clangor

hammer from the thicket's throat.
A doe, pregnant, her mouth webbed
with foam, foot pinned to her side, rides

snapping muscles, uphill tearing blind
out of a half-lit gully, and like heaven
bends to the stomped out smoke.

Buffalo Creek

Some black words, black as good soil,
blacker than bull calves blocking the road
where trucks idle, blacker than the oil
belly of a thunderhead, unload

wine-black the scouring rain,
and deluge is the answer.
Some words are coup de main,
and some canker,

snipped aluminum signs, sharp wager
that the ends justify the means,
a hitch in the governor's swagger
before he begins.

Some words can snuff, like day will night,
the lie in the nest the blue jay robs.
Some words are white

and when they blow, a wall thirty-foot high
bolts down the hollow like a cannonball
and men and women die.

Killing Frost

Frost diamond-scratched the panes,
the tarp's exterior dew frozen stiff.
Our Sadie licked a leathery pile
in the morning glitter: half-born pups,

all dead I wouldn't believe; I yelled
for Dad to help. He knew, without
bending a knee, removing a glove,
the batch was cold, and weren't ours.

She must have found them in the woods.
They looked like hers. She guarded
them even as he gently snagged
with the wide-mouthed coal shovel

the blue hairless thoughts I shared
with her. We reached the field's limit.
He laid the shovel like a nurse might
a blanket on the fulcrum of his shoulder.

The field waited, and Sadie waited,
and I held her collar to keep her,
as he flung them through the buds
damaged, frostbit, ice-tipped. She must

have found them in the woods,
I thought too late that morning
when the world grew thousandfold.
She must have found them in the woods.

School Bus Brocade

Now snow wets the squeaking black
floor of a bus. Always ten, she kicks
her boots, her backpack leans
between us. Rectangular windows
fog. In ours I draw an Arctic line,
finger-wide, ice-wet, as we leave
one stop for another. Like this dream,
a sparrow streak of light sidewinds
east, and when I curve the line
down, like this, towards the
window's silver ledge: green-grey,
red-brown, beautiful, even as
we speed to where we risk
we can't return.

To connect this viewless ride—
this core rattling teeth shudder,
rear tire chains biting
frozen highway—to where she
has gone, a route I can neither
be on nor refuse, is light
balancing the slope of two points
before the wheels move. Who

reaches to wipe the window's
compass in the passing buzz
pinetrees guardrails cowfence
laurel

Monongahela, Allegheny Coal Field . . .

The season turned them out on their heads.
The kids flicked butts at the tipple and tracks,
with Waylon on the radio, shirtsleeves cut free,
and blew through quick as pickups slipping
the valves of some mountain trumpet, rising
chord on chord like pines, like blasted fill,
high lonesome sound of high school football fields,
and higher still, shrinking in the belly of the air

over a city or Great Lake unknown to these
horizons strung three times, tree to tree.
Near the wasp-spangled tool shed, paper
bloat of an August harvest, someone regretted
each and every year he held onto them like a stone
turning in his belly. He held the answer,
heard the burden once lifted in the wind:
they be gone for good, no chance they stay.

Who Comes for Keeps

You reek of gashes in the woods after rain, after first October sun
rouses the corrugated iron. The porch snakes, spines shed,
whose tongues splinter your dovetailed corners, snakes who bored
deeper the mazes of rodents, the leaf-matted hair of oncoming winter,
won't flinch when a shotgun fuse trips bang: woods church-silent,
top of a transformer in there smoking. How would they not
bury themselves in your moist throw and sleep?

Mines open-throated as mountain singers, valleys scoured,
oak trees cured in the milky clouding flyrock the striplings lash.
They were never your four horses. A boy looks up from a clump
of agro-lime abandoned for years. "Did you hear that blast?"
Men squint their eyes at topographical maps; the boy will name
the startled cattle, the silhouette of a groundhog on the field,
and, below the field, trace for them the contour of your red hem.

It seemed like Mercy at the time. Remember when they broke in
their saddles as if to do a simple job, remember the scrape of skin.

Appalachia Grotesque

Drop from your shoulders the sky
        purpling down a scented
hayfield my buddies and I
        strode rowdy in blaze orange:

we plied the thicket for
        blighted chestnut, walnut,
seedhusk's bursting rapture,
        and the union sought;

how low our rifles swung
        parting unmown meadows,
our hips and thighs collecting
        dew, branches unshaken.

In the brakes
        we were boys and would
set fire to our mistakes—
        couldn't help it, Mother.

The leaning grass I seized,
        the thin roots kissed and drove
my hands across your knees
        born in the bark's black

sibilant cataract.

        Drop the sky, and while
I hold you, spill and lie back

        in the crook of a maple

blistered, ripe—

        only promise your key fruit

           and crown me in your lap.

My Uncle in Eden

A braid of snakes the water pipes warmed alive
lifted their diamond heads to lick the beads
strung below our feet, coaxing, unbeknownst,
the conviction that every choice is shed-able,
viviparous conversion where before

a peeling porch was just a peeling porch,
behind a furnace door nothing waiting.
My uncle slept on the couch, unmanned,
unemployed, his mind a burnt tin egg,
his Harley-Davidson for sale tarpaulined

in the sloughed spines of a Chinese chestnut.
We left him to waste in the black window
of his paralysis: a turning away for us,
a coming to terms for him. When offered
next to nothing we bailed for the Valley,

made good on our second chances.
We say we manage our resources best.

The Land of the Dead Is Open for Business

Take 22 from Pittsburgh International west through Weirton,

                                    cross the Ohio,

ride 7 all the way down.

                    To your left—barges, coal black with it.

Follansbee Coke Plant ignites the Night that never leaves that Other Shore.

A note in the margin of *1001 Love Poems,*
sincerity, intention pillowed in my younger hand,

                            and sequins,

her Sadie Hawkins taffeta caught on a latch
stuffed in a cedar box for twenty years,

                         or the folded swatch of childhood,

scented linoleum past
nicked from the sewing room floor

                  where she draped her shoulders

                        over the threshold,

and the part of her body with me a stranger—
she cranes her neck to guard the black shape of her parents' closed door:

                  now, she says.

Nothing's eternal in the land of the dead.

And after dinner, stars, vaulting heavens collated in the ridge-black
trees and portals' whirring fans, break my easy phrases:

> all my *Beauty-should-be-less-for-being-here.*
> Sad, lake hanging from the quicksilver air
> quivering . . .

I am writing in the dark an explanation

why this place doesn't black itself out, become a necklace of pylons
spanning Richmond to Cincinnati.

> Autobiography of cross-throughs, cuttings, pretense:
is this the way you see it,
the further you drift,
> the way a man

driving miles of border between a Palace and his home
along a silver road admits
who is Beloved, who is not,

            pulls to the median, radio off,
and awaits the heat of his shock to rise from the wheel,
                    and for his wrists to un-stiffen and lift

like a sound in his throat he cannot clear?

Richard's Story

Something startled the horses out of winter—
buckets, sugar tap, ice-covered salt lick;
a man collapsed on metal runners dragged
his balled-up fists in snow—two lines, his face
blue and deepening blue hauled through the hollow.
The mares, looked for from a kitchen window,
processed their Revelation over the white
and stopped in yellow flowers, stupid-eyed,
tonguing their bits. The sound of shaken tack
the only sound, this winter garden birdless,
and the boy waking someone up beside
the stove, her cries, a dog's upended dream
in a thicket. —It was an old, old story, he said.
Sunflowers, he said, swayed golden in the drifts,
what he had planted once and come up since.

Report, Upper Big Branch Mine Disaster

Beds and boots await the morning
light, gravel-clack, air pulsing
over teeming barns. Beware—

the wind will thicken with them,
strike squarely the legislator's eye,
finger his intake of breath,

refuse all circumlocution.
New mantrips hum, and a doe
slips through the mountain pass,

as tin-roofed houses shiver under
the euphemism *wrongful death*.
From the hillside's bristling,

the wind will thicken with them,
indict the chief executive
hoisted in his treestand of thought.

Wheeling Baptism

Down on an island tear-shaped as christ's sandal
fording the river, the flood-stage crests,
would wash the sinners under were it not
for the buckle of I-70 clasping Bridgeport.

Front Street's empty storefronts, white,
shin-deep in the cataclysm of their place,
sway to furtive preachers, lurch at whatever
wisps below—tins of negatives, paddlefish ribs,

the long dark train maneuvering spring
thaw through cores of cinder blocks,
squares of light clogged with sediment
they roll away in morning like a son.

The Famous Leap of Major McColloch's Horse

The spectacle you made of leaving her
rides you up black Wheeling Hill,
                              dogs the insignificant
creek—no matter how long the rain pounds,

nothing
but the Ohio is the Ohio.
                              Escape: a wet coat
lather in a summer bloodbath, a bit slips
like a broken bone in a mouth—

anything worn became your pair of wings.

The spars of trees tilt in pine darkness.

Can't take it back. Flight grows indefinite
in the telling,
what springs down a slope

painted no-matter-how
dizzyingly homerical

is cruel disregard, and then, as now, deserves
exact but brief analysis.

The spectacle you made of leaving her
rides you up black Wheeling Hill,

                      and rides you down.

A Marcellus Shale Primer

This cut swath languishes a century.
Opportunistic as men, rhododendrons
unfurl their livelihoods. I'm one of them

shut-in poets, who like birds bitch
their sunlight catches in the industry of plants
(from the safety of their sheltering therein),

and I hook commas deep in the bedrock-paydirt.

The Assumption

In short, my life has been a great one.
— *former Massey Coal CEO Don Blankenship*

A lead horse hangs his head.
      Reins and harness slip.
Tillage waits like dead
      Don Blankenship.

Whose lions leap the hogsbacks?
      Whose river overruns
The coal train on her tracks?
      No one's. No one's.

The worm sleeps in a rose,
      A hunter in the blind,
And when the shutters close
      For only wind,

Dogs dig up a churchyard,
      Dividing what they own,
And a poet scribbles mad
      Don's name in stone.

Down crooked letters plough
  Our crooked revery,
All lives are short—not how
  We should be.

Mercy Prayer

The hills tire of propping
what's left, dream to be
a tract-less plain
combed by the wind,
long like bored boys
in Cameron High's Vo-Ag
for a gun, a treestand,
last night's girl scent
lingering. They cup
their hands, stay warm,
breathe deeply, know
the cost of staying
the cost of Pittsburgh
is no alternative.
Hunker down here
like a burial mound
on the river. They know
a blindness that strikes
hunters before dawn,
a coy light when deer
come best. Some lose
their bearing in the mill,
the arc torch, icy roof,
some fall from trees

and break their necks.
I'm driving to her
down the ridge, hear
always a hummingbird's
stutter on the wind-
shield, gravel under tires.
Spin us—oh World—
spin us a second time,
out Grapevine, out Saltlick,
wield us light.

For as Long as It Lasts (and It Will Last If Money Can Be Made)

Vega declines west over Kayford Mountain,
the blasting at dawn. Even the Assyrians—
astronomers who tracked the same star
to predict in hopeless certainty the length
of a queen's life, the quality of that life,
and in whose death the blank sky shook—
would be at a loss to imagine such loss:
wildflowers scooped from underfoot, beating
dens choked with fill, manganese streams;
graveyards remain, and the birds who visit
on steles sometimes singing. What will you
do now that you know? A company truck
emblazoned in white dust descends dumbly
towards the sacrificed. The crowns of light
drift westerly, and the katydids' filamentous
monument, and the rocks' wild overburden,
and the draglines swoop and spill.

Benwood Mine and Queen Anne's Lace

Seven miles inside a hill
a man is rocking on his heels.
     His family calls him from the air,
     the sweet blue air too bright to breathe.
The lion and the doe are one;
we're waiting for the drill to come.

To lift a man into the air
is lighter than his mother's stare
     or prayers his children falcon up,
     unless the mountain hold him still,
a sleeping dove across the chest
as the preacher leaves us blessed:

"Our land is like a broken bottle
with the Truth inside, or flowers
     pressed for ages in a pit,
     or men interred behind a stone—"
Daughter turns her face away
before the Governor can say.

The sun is black behind the ridge
and cables countering the bridge.
     The river slips a noose around

        our waterfront's new blacktop lot
like coal inside a flower's pit.
We love the world in spite of it.

Even Windrows

Scattered names. The enslaved
were meant to be forgotten here.

He ploughs the grave markers
crossing windrows in the field.

Stones don't distinguish a man
from a burnt down Baptist church,

and they fall before the mainshare.
What could he tell his daughter?

Her calloused hands reach from
the flatbed for the weight he hoists;

a decade later children call it
Graveyard Field. It grew.

Her whirring blade cut sapling,
thistle, rodent, snake,

and drifted over the mouths
of dens penitent in darkness.

Two Doves Gone When He Was Gone (Windmills of Grief)

There is no heaven, but tall grasses
shimmer the wind, milk-heavy with seed.
The field lifts a wing.

She wrings a cloth in cold dishwater,
brushes with the back of her wrist
an eyelash, and lets the caravan arrive
joyless as an Apostle.

Her porch rings with "The King of Love
My Shepherd Is," with what they've read
of comforting, *the iron stylus and the rock,*

fruit basket cellophane, tupperware steaming
with the balm of pierogies. She hugs each
man and woman thank you and sees them off.
A tiny thing

flits yellow and black, renewing farewell.
The clothesline jumps.
Behind tired clouds the crows imagine human lives.

Vertical Blinds

In Medford bedrooms women, fingers twisting
the washed history of their hair, let mornings lengthen
   on windowsills, on empty walks, always the invisible

inconsolate sunlight marries another to the sea.
   The rose of island-impermanence zigzags from
the bay—wharves, rows of trees, clotheslines—,

   a skirt ripples darkly in an avenue of salt.
He holds fast, *couldn't return the same*,
   convinced himself, from the start, of anything:

a bark tacks towards the headland, flexing silver
   on a slip of the tide's scrubbed aluminum.
He clasps the ropes. Water slaps the bilge.

I Dream I Meet Irene McKinney at the Ruined House of the Photographer

Step inside, the air is heavy wet
newsprint or scent of vinegar, walls
graffitied and barely lit. It's time to go.
I tell her what she means to me, or try.
Quick as spit she pulls us up the stairs,
carpeted in the casings of beetles age-soft.
Birds cry, sweep through smother of twig and leaf.
Whole floors heave, her foot is past the landing;
some treads hold nestlings, some snakeslick.
At any moment I might falter, fall through,
hide my face, manage to bark, "no more,"
as she hauls us, winded, into a room
of portraits. She doesn't blink or look aside:
she's like their subjects, like the open bureau,
a room hidden in a house, called on at last,
windows thrown wide for years to catch this light.

Five String

Coal sings somewhere inside
us fathers. A black furnace

blesses our kids, buries
mountainlike vows, and the rest

banjoing between midwives
your new discord. Claw

the bridge, or burn
what your girl tomorrow

will hear. Thread that thought
(you have no choice),

peg it, tighten
so it twitches with the heat

of choice. You'll touch
that stirring until blisters.

Acknowledgments

The author would like to thank the editors of the following publications in which versions of these poems have appeared, some under different title:

12 Days of Fiction; Agni Online; Appalachian Heritage; Blackbird; The Boston Globe; The Center; Forklift, Ohio; The Harlequin; Jam Tarts Magazine; Poetry Northeast; Quiddity International; Salamander Magazine; Solstice; Southern Humanities Review; Unsplendid.

In addition, "Report, Upper Big Branch Mine Disaster" was made into a book by artist Laraine Armenti and exhibited at the Anderson University Jessie C. Wilson Galleries.

Thank yous

Thank you for your voices and support: Frederick Speers, Rachel
DeWoskin, Jeffrey Pethybridge, Kirun Kapur, Davide Adriano Nardi,
Sophie Powerstrong, Kate Snodgrass, K. Alexa Mavromatis, Marc
Olivere, Jennifer Kellner-Muscar, Mario Muscar, Michael Iafrate,
Kelly Strautmann, Clint Sutton, Richard and Roni Schotter, Laraine
Armenti, Martha Rhodes, Ryan Murphy, Clarissa Long, Lucie Brock-
Broido, Carolyn Forché, Robert Pinsky, John Whitehead, Derek
Walcott, Rosanna Warren, Marc Harshman, and Mom & Dad. Thank
you, Carolina Ebeid, for inviting me to the haire-brain'd counsel. A
special thank you to Louise Akers for questioning every line. Thank
you to the Massachusetts Cultural Council and the Hyla Brook Poets.
Thank you, Valerie Duff, for our partnership and for your voice in
every poem.

Raised in Marshall County, WV, Jacob Strautmann is a recipient of the Massachusetts Poetry Fellowship from the Massachusetts Cultural Council. His poems have appeared in the *Boston Globe, Agni Online, Salamander Magazine, Southern Humanities Review, Blackbird*, and others. He is the managing director of Boston Playwrights' Theatre at Boston University, where he also teaches creative writing. He lives in Belmont, MA with his partner Valerie Duff and their two children.

Publication of this book was made possible by grants and donations. We are also grateful to those individuals who participated in our 2019 Build a Book Program. They are:

Anonymous (14), Sally Ball, Vincent Bell, Jan Bender-Zanoni, Laurel Blossom, Adam Bohannon, Lee Briccetti, Jane Martha Brox, Anthony Cappo, Carla & Steven Carlson, Andrea Cohen, Janet S. Crossen, Marjorie Deninger, Patrick Donnelly, Charles Douthat, Morgan Driscoll, Lynn Emanuel, Blas Falconer, Monica Ferrell, Joan Fishbein, Jennifer Franklin, Sarah Freligh, Helen Fremont & Donna Thagard, Ryan George, Panio Gianopoulos, Lauri Grossman, Julia Guez, Naomi Guttman & Jonathan Mead, Steven Haas, Bill & Cam Hardy, Lori Hauser, Bill Holgate, Deming Holleran, Piotr Holysz, Nathaniel Hutner, Elizabeth Jackson, Rebecca Kaiser Gibson, Dorothy Tapper Goldman, Voki Kalfayan, David Lee, Howard Levy, Owen Lewis, Jennifer Litt, Sara London & Dean Albarelli, David Long, Ralph & Mary Ann Lowen, Jacquelyn Malone, Fred Marchant, Donna Masini, Louise Mathias, Catherine McArthur, Nathan McClain, Richard McCormick, Kamilah Aisha Moon, James Moore, Beth Morris, John Murillo & Nicole Sealey, Kimberly Nunes, Rebecca Okrent, Jill Pearlman, Marcia & Chris Pelletiere, Maya Pindyck, Megan Pinto, Barbara Preminger, Kevin Prufer, Martha Rhodes, Paula Rhodes, Silvia Rosales, Linda Safyan, Peter & Jill Schireson, Jason Schneiderman, Roni & Richard Schotter, Jane Scovell, Andrew Seligsohn & Martina Anderson, Soraya Shalforoosh, Julie A. Sheehan, James Snyder & Krista Fragos, Alice St. Claire-Long, Megan Staffel, Marjorie & Lew Tesser, Boris Thomas, Pauline Uchmanowicz, Connie Voisine, Martha Webster & Robert Fuentes, Calvin Wei, Bill Wenthe, Allison Benis White, Michelle Whittaker, Rachel Wolff, and Anton Yakovlev.

21st Century Policing

COMMUNITY POLICING

A Guide for
Police Officers
and
Citizens

By Sergeant Steven L. Rogers

LOOSELEAF LAW
PUBLICATIONS, INC.
P.O. BOX 650042, Fresh Meadows, NY 11365-0042
(718) 359-5559 *also* 24-hour Fax (718) 539-0941
www.LooseleafLaw.com   e-mail: llawpub@erols.com

Library of Congress Cataloging-in-Publication Data

Rogers, Steven L., 1951-
    21st Century policing : community policing : a guide for
police officers and citizens / by Steven L. Rogers.
        p.   cm.
    Includes index.
    ISBN #1-889031-18-6 (Paperback)
    1. Community policing—United States.   I. Title.
HV7936.C83R64 1998
363.2'3'0973—dc21   98-29880
                                                    CIP

ATTENTION: CORPORATIONS AND SCHOOLS
Looseleaf Law Publications, Inc. offers quantity discounts for educational,
business, or sales promotional use. For information, please call Looseleaf
Law Publications, Inc., (800) 647-5547.

This book is dedicated to the greatest
peacekeeping force in the history of mankind
— *The American Police Officer* —

TABLE OF CONTENTS

INTRODUCTION

THE LEGITIMATE OBJECT OF GOVERNMENT IS TO DO FOR A COMMUNITY
OF PEOPLE WHATEVER THEY NEED TO HAVE DONE, BUT CANNOT AT ALL
DO IN THEIR SEPARATE AND INDIVIDUAL CAPACITIES.

Abraham Lincoln

From the day we enter elementary school we are taught that in order to preserve our precious freedoms we must assume responsibility for our own actions and that of our freely elected government.

The conditions of our cities and towns insofar as infrastructure, environment, law and order is concerned depends on how each citizen chooses to impact public policies affecting the community in which he or she lives.

From 1776 to the middle of the twentieth century, Americans have always made it a point to become involved with community programs designed to enhance their quality of life. However, for reasons which are difficult to explain, Americans today are losing their will and desire to commit themselves to supporting the core values which have kept our nation as one country under God with liberty and justice for all.

The result of this lack of resolve to "get involved" has caused this nation to wander onto a very dangerous road which is leading to a time when chaos in our cities will replace law and order; when people will turn to committing violence at a rate like at no other time in history; and when policing as we know it today will be replaced with a policing none of us in this nation would want to see become a reality.

Until the American people and their leaders are willing to address in a very decisive manner the crime problems all of us face we better prepare for the future with the understanding that the worst is yet to come.

Blaming the courts, the police, the political establishment and every organization and person known to speak out on law enforcement issues has never in the past, not now, and will not in the future lead to the solutions which will solve our public safety problems.

To succeed in our mission to maintain safe streets we must commit ourselves to the goal of eliminating the opportunity for individuals to commit criminal acts and to recognize and admit that there exists one major element which has eroded our law enforcement efforts for the past thirty years. That element being — the strained relationship between the police and the people.

Public suspicion of the police is at an all-time high. Confidence in law enforcement is being shattered by numerous highly visible and well-publicized events like the Rodney King incident where police were video taped using excessive force; the O.J. Simpson trial where the police investigation was publicized as being amateur and inept; and the WACO compound disaster where police used an unprecedented amount of fire-power to apprehend individuals who violated federal laws; all of which tarnished the image of law enforcement nationwide. No matter what our individual personal opinions are of the police or the people involved in highly publicized incidents, it is clear that law enforcement is on trial and the evidence gathered against it does not look good.

The question we must find an answer to is: How do we fix what has become a broken relationship between the people and the police?

Many law enforcement experts say the answer can be found only through the support of community policing partnerships.

Until all of us awaken to the important role police-community relations has in our society and in some small way make a contribution to America's fight against crime pro-actively, more blood, sweat and tears, will flow in our streets, schools and homes like never seen before in our nation's history.

Fighting crime has been used as a political issue giving politicians a very popular campaign platform during election years. Politicians give good speeches and support well-intentioned programs in their efforts to show the people they are concerned with the public safety problems we are all facing. But the issues of crime fighting should not be discussed only during an election year or only when crime hits close to home. Crime in America poses a very clear and present danger to the existence of our society and the maintenance of our freedoms. Hence, community policing should not be viewed as just another political issue; it is actually an issue with such profound impact on law enforcement that our survival as a nation is at stake.

Policing methodologies implemented in the next century will determine where we as a nation will be going insofar as our freedom is concerned. If we fail to address the crime problems we face today, it is highly possible that the problems we face tomorrow will dwarf twentieth-century crime, thus eroding some of our precious freedoms.

Community Policing has a track record of enabling the police and the people to effectively address crime problems by forging together a potent force through proactive crime fighting partnerships.

This book provides citizens and police officers alike with the foundational blocks necessary to forge ahead in building a positive and productive working relationship with each other by advancing law enforcement efforts as we enter the next century. Community Policing is America's last hope to win the fight against crime.

Sergeant Steven L. Rogers

CHAPTER 1

POLICE LEADERSHIP
IN THE 21st CENTURY

LEADERSHIP IS INTANGIBLE, THEREFORE NO WEAPON EVER DESIGNED
CAN REPLACE IT.   *General Omar Bradley*

Leadership in the police profession carries with it responsibilities unlike any other occupational field. The decisions police supervisors and patrol officers make daily have direct impact on the people who live and work in the community they serve.

On a grander scale, the decisions law enforcement officers and administrators make directly impact on the public policies affecting our entire criminal justice system from local to national levels of government. To a great degree every decision determines how law enforcement agencies are addressing our crime problems today.

The most difficult leadership problems law enforcement supervisors confront each and everyday emanates from within the law enforcement organization itself. Low morale, a lack of productivity, apathy and numerous other problems affecting overall police performance are but a few internal issues that police supervisors must address.

During the past thirty years much has been said about the various reasons why "in-house" police problems exist. However, the common problem which a large number of law enforcement agencies share is the failure of upper management and middle supervisory personnel to effectively lead. The burden of this failure rests solely on the shoulders of those who occupy the highest levels of management. It is ultimately their responsibility to place the right people in the right positions to do the right job.

A 1997 survey of numerous New Jersey police officers of all ranks revealed that many officers recognize that leadership problems exist in their individual police agencies. These officers blamed upper police management's failure to establish management processes designed to enhance continuity in decision-making and in enforcing policies which clearly define the scope and mission of the organization.

Interestingly, the survey reveals that common "leadership failures" in the police profession usually result in the self-creation of individual policy-making with differing leadership styles being implemented on each shift and in each police unit. As one officer explains, "in my city we have three different police departments, one for each shift."

Confusion, no direction, the lack of clearly defined goals and objectives, and differing views on how to enforce the law has turned what should be a shared vision into a shared nightmare.

This chaos results in different leadership styles fragmenting the rank and file, deteriorating discipline and order and eventually breaking down law enforcement effectiveness.

Just how this chaos is born is no secret to many officers who witness the deterioration internal problems cause their agencies. The overwhelming conclusion of police officers who have seen leadership fail in their agencies claim that "ivory tower" management is the cause.

Police managers who live in the "tower" rarely know what's happening on the streets of their community or in the ranks of those whom they are leading. Officers claim that supervisors never or rarely request their input, opinions, suggestions, or ideas when specific public safety problems must be addressed. Hence, the feeling among many rank and file police officers is that they are *apart from* instead of *a part of* the agency in which they are employed. They are saying that the leadership failures in law enforcement not only build walls between the police and the public; they also build walls between the police and the police.

Getting Out of the "Tower"

A WORD FOR POLICE MANAGERS AND SUPERVISORS

Getting out of the "ivory tower" and getting to know the men and women who work for you is the only way you will know what is on their minds and what is happening in the streets of your community. Second and third hand information will not suffice. Direct communication between the leader and the subordinate is the best advice any individual in a leadership position can take if he or she wants to be effective.

Many police officers differ on what they identify to be a good leader. However, the most common characteristics of a good leader is that person who gives his people a reason to care for their police agency and the people they serve. Good leaders induce followers to act for certain goals that represent the values and the motivations, the wants and needs, the aspirations and expectations of both leaders and followers. The genius of leadership lies in the manner in which supervisors act toward the people they interact with — be those people subordinates, other leaders or the citizenry.

If leaders are not motivated, subordinates will not be motivated. If leaders are not inspired, subordinates will not be inspired. Hence, supervisors who do not have leadership characteristics which inspire and motivate, are not leaders at all. Simply put, they are people with a title.

In police work, the wrong man or woman in a position of leadership, who lacks the fundamental characteristics and skills to lead, can bring upon a police department and an entire community disastrous consequences.

Effective Leadership & MBWA

The first step toward being an effective police department leader, be you a police chief or a police sergeant is to learn to use a leadership skill called "MBWA" — *Managing By Wandering Around.* This leadership skill is used by police department leaders who are committed to motivating and inspiring their people.

Leaders using "MBWA" skills refuse to be trapped in the "ivory tower." They get their hands "dirty." They walk the talk and project a determination to include everyone as part of the team which is tasked to get the mission accomplished.

Abraham Lincoln knew what "MBWA" meant to the success of his administration both in peace and in war. He traveled on the field of battle to meet the troops and to hear their views and opinions about the war. Many times he made decisions based on what his men told him. Lincoln was a people president. He strongly believed in "MBWA" and instructed his military Generals to employ this skill in their decision-making process.

When Lincoln learned that General John C. Fremont didn't use the "MBWA" management skill and made the cardinal mistake of isolating himself from his men, allowing no one to see him, Lincoln fired him. Fremont did not know what was going on in the very high matter he was dealing with and lost not only the confidence of his men and the president, but also lost numerous battles.

United States Army General George Patton and General Douglas MacArthur employed the "MBWA" policy on the field of battle and enjoyed astonishing victories because their men respected them like no other military leaders in history. The same was true for a general who has been called America's most beloved military leader, Robert E. Lee.

Leaders who put their people first and inspire by example are winners! Take care of the people who work for you and they will take care of you. "MBWA" is being in-touch with patrol officers and the people who live and work in the community. "MBWA" facilitates innovation and strengthens law enforcement core values which could mean the very survival of the police organization and its overall effect on public safety.

Leadership is an influence process dependent upon the relationship between leaders and followers. Getting things done through others implies a process of people working together to achieve shared goals and aspirations. One element that differentiates leaders from others is that leaders have a vision for the mission to be accomplished. Leaders place matters in perspective. They have a vision for the future and know in order for their leadership to be effective and successful their vision must be shared.

Good police leaders know who they are and where they and the organization are going. They are self-starters, knowledgeable and confident. They have the ability to infuse important transcending values into an enterprise.

FOUR LEADERSHIP SKILLS FOR THE
EFFECTIVE POLICE SUPERVISOR

- **The skill to communicate**. Communication is an art. Effective police leaders have to be skilled mediators and negotiators. They have to be diplomats, be able to stir things up, encourage an exchange of ideas, interaction and dialogue.

- **The skill to motivate**. This is accomplished by sharing the vision and co-creating the vision.

- **The skill to empower**. This is accomplished by delegating authority.

- **The skill to take risks**. Keep in mind that the risk-takers in life are the ones who usually succeed.

An Effective Leader in Police Work Will:

- Initiate Performance
- Work Well With Others
- Embrace Change
- Do the Job
- Build Trust
- Communicate Well
- Identify with Followers/Subordinates
- Extend Vision

A good police department is not led by a man who is given a title to simply occupy an office. A good police department is led by a man who hears the people on the streets and the officers under his command. He understands them, unites them, directs them to a common goal, inspires them, motivates them and gives them a sense of ownership and purpose. Such is the leader who leads a great police department.

CHAPTER 2

EMBRACING CHANGE

HE WHO REJECTS CHANGE IS THE ARCHITECT OF DECAY.
Prime Minister Harold Wilson

During the past decade law enforcement practitioners concluded that very poor or non-existent police-community relations coupled with the constant flow of negative publicity about police misconduct, corruption and excessive use of force resulted in an erosion of public confidence in law enforcement nationwide.

In 1996, there was general agreement among law enforcement officers from throughout America that police administrators who ignored internal problems which continuously eroded the morale and performance of police personnel allowed their agencies to become ineffective and an embarrassment to the entire law enforcement community.

By the end of 1996, problems related to police image became a priority in many police departments resulting in an aggressive campaign to change the image of policing by addressing long ignored problems related to how police interacted with the general public. This campaign lead police agencies across America to change their traditional policing methods to a more advanced methodology by introducing to their communities proactive community policing methodologies to problem-solving processes. The introduction of Community Policing not only meant a re-evaluation of how the police interacted with the community, but also how the police interacted with the police.

The seventies and eighties gave birth to police subcultures; commonly known as "five-percenters" — officers who are identified in the police rank and file as individuals who compromise their oath of office by their misconduct. "Five-percenters" usually apply peer pressure on good officers and encourage them to be part of the so-called "wall of silence" when illegal activity is being investigated.

One unfortunate element the law enforcement profession suffers from is the high number of police officers who choose to remain silent when they witness police corruption, brutality and other actions embarrassing the police profession.

Why good cops protect bad cops by their failure to act against their misconduct is a mystery which can only be solved by the individual officer who is confronted with a situation challenging his integrity. Fortunately, as the mid-nineties passed, the "blue wall of silence" in many police agencies began to crumble because Community Policing began to impact the police community before it impacted the civilian population.

Community Policing brings to the surface good cops who are tired of being stigmatized and stereotyped as bad cops because of the bad behavior of the few. One by one, good cops are addressing the "five-percenter" problem by not yielding to peer pressure and by refusing to keep silent when witnessing police misconduct.

In early 1997, the police profession employed better educated police officers who filled the ranks of patrolman to chief. Many of these officers decided to police their own community; i.e., their own ranks. The subsequent result has been a more positive public image.

Although the "five-percenter" movement is on the decline, a new sub-culture is on the rise. This subculture consists of officers who oppose anything a police administrator will do to progress towards the department's goals and objectives. These officers generally do not compromise their oath of office, but their lack of vision and apathetic behavior nonetheless erodes morale and productivity.

These officers are called "negatrons" — meaning, everything they see, touch or smell is viewed as a negative factor and thus must be opposed. They create the "us against them" attitude and usually use peer pressure to support their influences.

"Negatrons" surface on two levels of the police organization. The first is the supervisory level — patrol sergeants to be specific. Without the support of patrol supervisors it is near impossible for police administrators to implement changes in policy. "Negatrons" on the supervisory level work hard to hinder positive change. They are apathetic, lack vision and fail to understand the need for change.

The second level of negatrons exist in the rank and file of street cops. These men and women are usually narrow-minded, live in a fantasy that police work is like what they see on television and lack the much-needed education which is required to effectively serve the public and combat crime as we enter into the 21st century. Negatrons are the architects of decay in the police profession.

For police executives to effectively implement community policing methodologies they must first address the elements in their agencies which serve no purpose but to hinder quality policing. If these elements are not addressed, the spread of "negatronism" and the rebirth of "five-percenters" will become a reality and eventually erode every effort to maintain respectable, professional standards in law enforcement.

As we move towards the 21st century challenges in policing will require police executives to make dramatic and sweeping changes in recruitment procedures, police academy training, in-service training and department management policies. These challenges cannot be addressed overnight. They can be successful only if police department leadership maintains a determination to bring about positive change.

CHAPTER 3

ADDRESSING PROBLEMS

IGNORING THE PROBLEMS WE FACE TODAY WILL SURELY RESULT IN
DISASTER TOMORROW.   *Sgt. Steven Rogers*

Image problems permeate police agencies all across the nation. When one police agency receives negative press the entire profession suffers. An illustration of how far-reaching problems can affect the profession as a whole is the string of bad press the Los Angeles Police Department received in 1996 and 1997.

The infamous Rodney King incident and O.J. Simpson trial caused a national outrage not only against the Los Angeles Police Department but also against police in general across America. Making matters worse were the fiascos created by federal law enforcement agencies. First, was an incident in the west where a teenager and his mother were shot by federal agents; then the WACO, Texas incident, where the A.T.F. used tanks, bombs and helicopters instead of common sense in addressing a local public safety problem. When police overreact and the result is the death of innocent people, public confidence in law enforcement erodes rapidly, not only in the eyes of the general public but also in the ranks of police officers themselves.

The Issue of Police Image
Global vs Local

How does a police chief in a large city or small town address the every day internal problems which have the potential to cause public confidence in his police department to erode? This question is one with which numerous police administrators are constantly burdened.

Unfortunately, not many police administrators realize the "global" impact of their failure to address policy and personnel problems. When serious infractions by police personnel are ignored by police management the signal being communicated to department personnel is one which is usually interpreted as administrative apathy — "if they don't care why should I." This attitude spreads departmentwide and eventually erodes discipline and good order, thus affecting police performance.

The solution to many internal problems is for police management to act swiftly when a serious problem surfaces. For example, in 1995 a case involving two New York City police officers who allegedly beat a dog to death was widely publicized and caused much public scorn. When NYPD Commissioner Bill Bratton learned of the incident he took swift action and fired the officers.

In that same year a Midwestern police officer beat a Baptist minister with the butt of a shotgun and another officer with the same department beat a priest with a nightstick.

The police chief acted immediately and fired one cop and suspended the other. Although many rank and file officers protested, the chief stood his ground and sent a strong message to other problem officers — if you compromise your oath of office, you will lose your job!

In a Southeastern American city, a number of police officers resisted their chief's new policies which required accountability and discipline. His remedy resulted in command positions being shuffled, officers with consistent behavioral problems suspended and officers who refused to support management changes in policing methodologies were given a choice — resign or get fired. Within thirty days this police department changed from one of complacency to one of pride and productivity.

The local problems each of these law enforcement agencies faced became "global" for the entire police profession. It is important to keep in mind that if a police officer on the west coast is arrested for corruption, the image of the officers on the east coast will also suffer.

Preventing Local Problems From Becoming Global

Several years ago the Kansas City Police Department developed a system which flags cops having problems communicating with the public. Citizen complaints are tracked by a computer which flags any officer with three or more complaints against him in a six-month period. Problem officers are required to meet with division commanders who have the discretion to refer them to a communications course. Communications skills are addressed in such a way that police officers learn that communication is about tone, pitch and body language as well as verbal.

It is not just talking, it is also listening. Officers learn about the different signals they communicate when they wear certain types of equipment and clothing, such as leather gloves, mirrored glasses and other traditional "Hollywood"-type place garb.

In other cities police are required to learn about the diverse cultures in their community in order to prevent communication problems from turning a minor incident into a major catastrophe. For example, sometime ago a newspaper reported that two police officers in the Midwest stopped a motorist who they believed was transporting weapons. After police ordered the driver to get out of his car they ordered him to fall to the ground. Instead of falling to the ground the driver began to run and ended up in a physical confrontation with police. Although no weapons were found the driver was arrested for assault. Prior to this incident the driver had no problems with police. In fact, hundreds of people, including police officers from the driver's community praised him as a quiet, law-abiding citizen.

An investigation into the matter found that the driver was from a South American nation where, when the police ordered you to the ground, they killed you. One can only imagine what would have happened if the police used poor judgment and employed lethal force. Hence, the importance of learning about the people who live and work in our communities.

CHAPTER 4

MANAGEMENT FAILURES

IT IS HARD TO FAIL, BUT IT IS WORSE NEVER TO HAVE TRIED TO
SUCCEED.   *Theodore Roosevelt*

There are two basic management failures common in most police
agencies. One is the failure to raise qualifications and standards;
the other failure is the belief that micro-management is a tool
which can get the job done.

In many states, individuals who seek to become a police officer
need only to possess a high school diploma or equivalent and they
must pass a written and/or oral examination. In many cases
standards are lowered to increase minority participation. And in
numerous jurisdictions political considerations are made regarding
recruitment of "connected" individuals.

Lowering standards and allowing politics to enter into the decision-
making process of police recruit selection has proven to be
disastrous for law enforcement. Unqualified and undereducated
people in the police profession has resulted in increased civil law-
suits, false arrest complaints, police brutality charges, corruption
and the spreading of a "siege" mentally in the rank and file.

Most police chiefs in America belong to a "Chiefs' Association"
where they can recommend changes in the selection process. Each
individual chief can exercise his executive power to establish
uniform standards for policing based on the public needs in his or
her community. As we approach the 21st century, chiefs of police
are going to have to raise their collective voices to address these
issues and maintain professional standards designed to attract
quality people to the law enforcement profession.

Qualification and recruitment standards should require police
candidates to have completed a minimum of two years of college
or one tour of duty in the U.S. military or civilian public service.

In addition, five basic educational requirements should be completed by police candidates. One, certification in multicultural studies; two, basic skills in a secondary language which dominates the candidates geographical area; three, family crisis intervention; four, English composition; and five, communication skills.

Police managers need to identify the officers in their department who lack the skills and training necessary to perform their duty effectively. With the implementation of community policing, communication skills, mediation skills and skills in diplomacy are very important policing tools for the officer of the 21st century.

In New Jersey, the New Jersey Community Policing Officers Association provides training in numerous community policing areas of study. The course is conducted by active police officers who volunteer their time to maintain professional standards in the law enforcement community.

Nearly fifty police departments took advantage of this training in 1997. Also, train the trainer courses have been created to give police chiefs the opportunity to have their best officers trained to train other officers. Additionally, in 1998, the Bergen County Community Policing Institute was created to certify police officers in community policing.

Micro-Management

Law enforcement managers who micro-manage lack vision and effective managerial skills which are necessary to promote team work, improve morale, increase productivity and encourage initiative. These managers are a liability to community policing programs.

Micro-managers always second guess their subordinates and manage through intimidation and fear. They fail to identify the strength of each officer which, if such strengths are identified, could be an asset to the police department.

Management By Objectives
and Autocratic Rule

Police administrators differ in the type of management styles they use. Many administrators continue to use the "management by objectives (MBO)" method while others use autocratic styles of management. Both the MBO and autocratic management styles have a proven track record of being ineffective when addressing community policing issues.

CHAPTER 5

TOTAL QUALITY LEADERSHIP
TOTAL QUALITY MANAGEMENT

IF WE DON'T LEARN FROM HISTORY, HISTORY IS BOUND TO REPEAT
ITSELF. *General Douglas MacArthur*

In order for a police department to maximize its effectiveness in community policing implementation, policymakers need to establish management criteria and policies similar to that of major corporations and most recently the United States Military. These organizations have integrated TQL/TQM into all management levels. The introduction of TQL/TQM methodologies in police management serves to prevent both internal and external problems from developing as well as improve police performance.

TQL/TQM policies are perhaps the most effective management skills being employed by police agencies to boost morale, increase productivity and create an atmosphere of harmony between management and police officers.

IMPLEMENTATION OF TQL/TQM

TQL/TQM is fairly easy to implement. Every day the Chief of Police holds a commander's call with his command staff. During this time he receives command staff briefings on events which occurred in the past 24 hours. When unusual or remarkable issues arise, the Chief seeks solutions by asking for input from his command staff. The command staff then shares these issues with patrol supervisors and seeks their opinions, ideas and input. Police supervisors then convene a "huddle group" at roll call where they speak with the officers on the street regarding important issues and encourage their input in solving problems. At the conclusion of the "huddle," supervisors forward any ideas or suggestions from patrol officers to the command staff who, in turn, forward same to the Chief for action.

When problems are so significant that they extend into the community, it is recommended that the TQL/TQM methodology be utilized as a tool to include citizens in the problem solving process. In this case, the community policing officers form neighborhood huddles.

The TQL/TQM-Huddle methodology invites total participation by police department personnel on all levels of the table of organization. In addition, public input is also welcome, thus sending a signal into the community promoting harmony, partnership and ownership between the police and the people.

TQL/TQM boosts morale, increases worker productivity, gives employees incentives to develop and suggest cost effective methods of problem-solving and encourages innovative thinking in addressing organizational goals and objectives.

The men and women who work on the streets know best the needs of the neighborhoods they patrol. TQL/TQM reveals the strengths of even the weakest performer in the organization, thus giving management the opportunity to foster those strengths more effectively.

The Table of Organization

With the introduction of TQL/TQM, it is important for the Police Chief to give his community policing supervisor direct access to him. Many times when community policing officers are required to go through numerous levels of command, things get lost and the response to public needs and wants is delayed.

Police administrators who have created community policing units and/or community policing as an integral part of the day to day operations of patrol bureau functions, have found that a chain of command which eliminates middle managers from the Community Policing Supervisor to the Police Chief is most effective.

CHAPTER 6

IMPLEMENTING COMMUNITY POLICING

A JOURNEY OF A THOUSAND MILES MUST BEGIN WITH A SINGLE STEP.
Chinese Proverb

A first major step for police administrators planning to implement community policing methodologies in his/her agency is to establish a mission statement and develop in-service training workshops for all police department personnel in order to give every officer the opportunity to learn about the scope and concept of community policing. Police personnel should know what community policing is, why it is being implemented, what is expected of them and what they are to expect from the citizens, the political establishment and the police administration.

Once police officers are familiar with department policy regarding community policing, the public must be made aware of the changes in policing that will be taking place in their community. This is accomplished through the creation of police-public partnerships which are discussed in more detail in Chapter 11.

Removing the Police Mystique

Once police personnel and the public are made aware of the merits of community policing, the police administration must take important steps to eliminate the "mystique" which surrounds law enforcement in general.

Most citizens complain that their police departments are isolated from them. There is a "mystique" which denies the public access to the "top brass" or specific information regarding the public safety of their community. Such a perception strengthens the wall of separation between the police and the public. People who complain about this "mystique" are right. What's the big secret?

You would think that some police departments are holding a secret nuclear war plan when people ask for access to information they are entitled to. Citizens need to be *a part of* not *apart from* the local law enforcement agency. In addition, the police complain that the people do not fully understand their job and have little or no sympathy for the problems they encounter daily.

In some cases, the people and the police have legitimate complaints. But, in most cases, these complaints are based on perceptions. Perceptions, however, are real in the eyes of the beholder and it is the responsibility of the police to take the necessary steps to change public perceptions from negative influences to positive influences.

This can be achieved by police management encouraging direct constructive dialogue between the Police Chief, department command staff, the officers on the beat and the people who live in the community.

Two Model Illustrations

In 1995, Nutley, New Jersey Police Chief Robert DeLitta organized quarterly "Town Hall" meetings where he and his key command staff officers met with the public in an informal open forum. During these meetings numerous public safety issues were discussed. These issues included patrol policies, police procedures regarding current issues affecting the community, policing methodologies and citizen complaints.

In that same year, Montclair, New Jersey Police Chief Thomas Russo began a program which encourages citizens to attend community policing in-service training courses for his police personnel. Numerous citizens who attended these sessions learned about the pressures and difficulties facing police officers today.

Both the Nutley Police Department and Montclair Police Department, over a period of time, eliminated the "mystique" surrounding their departments and opened the door for direct communication between the police and the public.

Your "Town Hall" Meeting
Where to Begin

Preparation

In order to organize an effective "Town Hall" meeting, it is recommended that the following steps be taken:

- Identify community problems which need to be addressed;
- Discuss these problems with command staff and patrol officers;
- Schedule your "Town Hall" meeting at a time and on a date convenient for the public;
- Publicize the date of the meeting in your local newspaper at least two weeks in advance;
- Set an agenda and emphasize that the free and open exchange of ideas, suggestions and constructive criticisms of the department are welcome;
- Have a citizen in the community moderate the meeting.

The Day of the Meeting

The Police Chief, his command staff and community policing officers should be present at the meeting. It is recommended that individuals representing political offices not participate. The presence of politicians tend to politicize the event, hence the reason for this suggestion.

The citizen moderator opens the meeting, establishes some ground rules and introduces the Police Chief. The Chief introduces his staff and briefly shares the purpose of the meeting with those in attendance. He briefly discusses current public safety issues affecting the community, crime statistics and other pertinent information. After sharing this information with the citizenry, he opens the meeting for public comments and discussion.

It is recommended that promises which cannot be kept, not be made. Follow-up on all complaints and other matters should be addressed within 24 hours. Credibility is established when action is taken within a reasonable amount of time.

CHAPTER 7

REORGANIZING PATROL OPERATIONS

I WALK SLOWLY, BUT I NEVER WALK BACKWARD.

Abraham Lincoln

As we approach the next century, police departments will be required to provide increased patrol coverage, better communications with the public and innovative policing methods to accomplish their mission to protect and serve their communities.

Traditionally, random patrol has been the operational method utilized by police departments in deploying officers into the community. However, during the past twenty years, studies on police operations in many areas of the nation have resulted in numerous police practitioners concluding that the effectiveness of random patrol is inadequate for policing communities in the future.

Random patrol restricts patrol officers to a reactive patrol mode which limits their contact with the public. Random patrol causes a visual problem known as "tunnel vision" which discourages police officers from conducting minor investigations, as well as from initiating positive interaction with the public. As a result of these disadvantages, the birth of community policing has become the choice many police agencies are taking in developing patrol operations.

Community policing gives police agencies the opportunity to change patrol operations from traditional random patrol methods to a more advanced and effective "directed patrol" methodology which enables patrol supervisors and their officers to actively engage in proactive problem-solving. This is accomplished by identifying community needs and problems, studying problem-solving options and taking the necessary steps toward accomplishing a desired result. When a solution to a specific problem is agreed upon, patrols are directed toward the problem area where increased interaction with the public and increased police visibility will decrease the potential for criminal activity. Directed patrols are deployed on foot, bicycle and motor vehicle.

The success of directed patrol depends upon the implementation of TQL/TQM methodologies. Police officers in neighborhoods know what the public safety needs of the community are and the "who's who" in each neighborhood.

DIRECTED PATROL
— The Three Tier Implementation Process —

Change does not come without some resistance. And most resistance to community policing emanates from police personnel. However, resistance from within the rank and file could be greatly reduced by using the TQL/TQM approach when implementing changes for community policing purposes.

Recommendations
— Implementation of Directed Patrol —

1. A written policy explaining standard operating procedures should be established by the Office of Chief of Police. The policy and S.O.P. should clearly define the purpose of directed patrol and its expected results.

2. Supervisory personnel should be briefed on the new patrol procedure and questions, ideas and other important dialogue should be encouraged.

3. Once supervisory personnel are informed of this new patrol method they, in turn, inform patrol division personnel of the new patrol procedures, and encourage input from them.

Directed Patrol
Operational Process

1. Patrol supervisors assign patrols to specific "troubled spots." Officers not assigned to specific "troubled spots" are encouraged to direct their patrols to areas they consider to be potential problems for the police. A problem is defined as any public concern brought to the attention of the police. For example, crime is obviously a policing problem. However, the community policing officer becomes a conduit for all problems the citizenry faces. Hence, the officer should be prepared to solve community problems as soon as possible. Some of the problems brought to the officer's attention may involve matters which need the attention of other municipal services such as the road department, tree department and other agencies outside the public safety department. Effective community policing requires interaction with numerous government and private services.

2. At the end of each tour of duty, supervisory personnel should debrief patrol officers for the purpose of discussing extra-ordinary incidents or specific public concerns which surfaced during the prior tour of duty. Officers should be asked for their input, ideas and suggestions on how to solve problems or address certain public needs brought to their attention.

3. Supervisors should discuss issues brought to their attention by patrol officers with department command personnel who, in turn, will brief the Police Chief, if necessary.

4. In the event a problem needs to reach a higher level of management, the Police Chief reviews the information, ideas, suggestions, etc., and develops a problem-solving action plan with his operations officers who forward the plan to patrol division personnel where directed patrol is implemented. This entire process works on a 24-hour basis. In other words, public needs are immediately addressed.

Foot Patrol — Without the Feet

Community policing means increased interaction with the public. Directed patrol provides direction and focus on specific community needs and problems. Combining both methodologies into community policing, directed foot patrol is born and becomes a very effective patrol operation in preventing crime.

Foot patrol was the choice of patrol in the early days of policing. However, with the introduction of high-tech police equipment, foot patrols became a thing of the past. As a result of increases in crime, many police practitioners have concluded that "high-tech robo cop" policing, which swept across America in the nineteen eighties, is doing little to address public safety needs in many urban and suburban areas. High-tech equipment is effective in combating crime from a reactive perspective; but all the electronic equipment on earth cannot address quality of life issues, racial conflict or economic collapse in neighborhoods where crime is running rampant. Those things are left to the community policing officer to address.

Many police administrators desire to implement foot patrols in their communities. However, because of manpower shortages and budget restraints, they are unable to commit men to perform this patrol operation. In other words, they don't have the feet necessary to walk the beat.

P.W.T.

Innovative police managers have overcome budget shortfalls and manpower problems by implementing an alternative program to foot patrols — Park-Walk-Talk (PWT) — a directed patrol method which requires police officers to park their patrol cars in the neighborhoods they are assigned or a specific area of their choice. These officers walk for no less than fifteen minutes per hour during which time they interact with businessmen, residents, merchants, children and every person they come in contact with. Park-Walk-Talk opens lines of communication between the police and the people thus enhancing positive police-community relations.

Vertical Patrol

Another cost effective patrol method is "Vertical Patrol" — a directed foot patrol procedure designed to increase police visibility in high-rise housing projects or apartment buildings.

Vertical Patrol Model

- Officers should be furnished with flyers and/or business cards to distribute to apartment residents and superintendents. This material identifies the officers to the residents and explains the Vertical Patrol program.

- Officers patrolling specific buildings should encourage public-police dialogue by interacting with residents. If a problem is brought to the officers' attention, appropriate action should be taken within 24 hours.

- Officers should perform this patrol operation in pairs and notify their communications center each time they enter a different floor or apartment.

- Patrolling apartment complexes on a one-per-week schedule is sufficient. Recommended times for Vertical Patrol are: 1000 to 1200 hours, 1300 to 1600 and 1900 to 2100 daily. Surprise visits should also be scheduled.

Each community has different public safety needs. Community policing enables the police officer on foot patrol to:

- increase his/her visibility,
- offer input in problem-solving,
- add a "human component" to policing in the community.

CHAPTER 8

QUALITY OF LIFE POLICING

LIFE IS NOT SO IMPORTANT AS THE DUTIES OF LIFE.

John Randolph

J. Q. Wilson's "broken windows" theory brought to the attention of police practitioners the link between quality of life issues and crime.

The infrastructures of our communities are falling apart and becoming breeding grounds for drug activity, gangs and other criminal elements. One sure way to prevent crime is to prevent the decay of our neighborhoods.

Interestingly, police officers are the only people who can quickly report a "broken window" for immediate action, thus proactively addressing potential crime problems. Once the "window" is repaired the probability of more windows being broken is diminished. This policing is called Quality of Life Policing (Q.L.P.).

As police officers patrol their assigned neighborhoods, they should be required to maintain a check list of infrastructure problems which have the potential of becoming public safety problems. For example, if a patrol officer notices that a store in his area of patrol has gone out of business and the building is empty, he should make note of it. If, after several weeks pass, the officer notices high grass, broken windows, broken down doors and general deterioration of the property, he should immediately contact the appropriate city agency for action. Q.L.P. prevents crime at its roots.

A Model Quality of Life Policing Project

In January of 1997, the New Jersey Police-Community Relations Officers Association, in partnership with the Montclair, New Jersey Police Department, mapped out a plan to clean up two Montclair neighborhoods plagued by crime and drug activity. The plan was put into action on April 26, 1997, when over 200 police officers and other volunteers from throughout New Jersey (including teens), "invaded" the crime-plagued streets targeted for clean up. In five hours, the infrastructure of these neighborhoods changed for the better. As a result of these volunteers collecting hundreds of pounds of debris, clearing empty lots, knocking down crack houses and replacing overflowing garbage cans with flower pots, these neighborhoods now belong to the people instead of the criminal elements who occupied the streets in the past.

A Step-by-Step Approach to Retaking the Streets
Montclair Project Unity

On November 21, 1996, the National Housing Institute, under the guidance of Mr. Ira Resnick convened a conference entitled: *Strengthening Families and Communities, the Role of Leaders and the Civil Society.* Attending this conference were representatives from several religious, housing, educational, business, government and law enforcement organizations.

Individuals attending the conference learned that a majority of people in our society have a strong sense that the core values which bond our communities together are eroding; that the character of our civil life is becoming endangered as a result of public apathy; that our political leaders have failed to commit themselves to strengthening our communities; that the will for people to volunteer their time to problem-solving is disappearing; and that the institutions which have kept our nation and our families strong are becoming weak. It became apparent to participants listening to people who live in areas where dealing with crime is a way of life that the cycle of economic erosion, violence and educational short-falls has not been adequately addressed.

One observation made at this conference was that not one elected municipal government official was in attendance. This absence of government representation clearly revealed that the political "will" to address problems plaguing our society is non-existent. "Politicians will establish committees, make speeches and make promises.

But here was an opportunity for them to look, learn and listen to the victims of government failure," noted one participant.

Interestingly, and with surprise, the people who spoke out on these crime issues expressed their belief that the police in their communities held the key to a successful campaign in addressing the problems they faced. It became apparent that the people maintained a strong sense of confidence in the police departments which institutionalized community policing in their communities.

The Genesis of the Montclair Project

The Montclair Project, named "Project Unity," is a people-problem solving community policing model which was conceived on November 21, 1996, after the conference described above was concluded.

On December 19, 1996, Nutley, New Jersey Police Sergeant Steven Rogers, President of the New Jersey Policing-Community Relations Officers Association and a participant in the November 21st conference sponsored by the National Housing Institute, decided to take decisive action on the problems he learned from the citizens who testified before a committee he was a member of. "It became very apparent that the people being most victimized by these problems had given up on political promise-makers and were now looking toward the police for solutions — specifically their Police-Community Relations Units," said Rogers.

The first thing Sergeant Rogers did was meet with Nutley Police Chief Robert DeLitta, President of the Essex County Association Chiefs of Police, to discuss a number of ideas he had regarding this issue. Chief DeLitta and the Sergeant discussed the overall problems affecting cities which had a ripple affect on towns like Nutley. DeLitta knew that crime is like a cancer. "If no one addresses the root causes of crime, it spreads and kills everything in its path," he said.

After reviewing a number of problem-solving options, DeLitta endorsed the Sergeant's proposal to initiate a project designed to address the problems affecting public safety from a global and local perspective. They developed five initial steps towards the problem-solving process:

- The first step in the process of finding solutions is to clearly define the "global" problem. In this case, criminal activity, as a result of economic collapse and the decay of core values, resulted in the erosion of neighborhoods which resulted in breeding grounds for small gangs and drug addicts to promote their criminal activity which had the potential of spreading beyond local boundaries.

- The second step is to scale down the "global" perspective to a "local" perspective and target a specific area plagued by many of the problems causing an escalation in crime.

- The third step is to select participants for the problem-solving process and develop goals, objectives and a mission statement.

- The fourth step is to develop a community policing and quality of life policing strategy for implementation.

- The fifth step is implementation.

The problem on a "global" scale was defined as *economic erosion resulting in deterioration of neighborhoods and finally an escalation in criminal activity.* "Locally" just about every major city in New Jersey has this serious problem.

On January 12, 1997, Mr. Ira Resnick of the National Housing Institute and Sergeant Steven Rogers met in Nutley, New Jersey to further discuss the problems learned at the conference of November, 1996. They developed a plan to deliver solutions to people affected by the problems discussed above. Both Resnick and Rogers agreed that the police held the power to make things happen in each community; but local police did not have the resources to undertake such a massive project. Hence, both men agreed that the only option left to proceed with the project was to call for volunteers from police agencies and the citizenry at large from throughout the state.

Rogers insisted that the police, via community policing units, take the lead in creating partnerships with local citizens. Resnick agreed, but expressed apprehension that police officers would (a) get deeply involved in such a project on a volunteer basis and (b) that the police would be well-received at a time when America's law enforcement community was recovering from highly-publicized police incidents which cast a negative image of law enforcement nationwide.

During discussions regarding the "police factor," Rogers agreed that there may be some merit to what Resnick was concerned about. He (Rogers) suggested that they convene a meeting of the New Jersey Community Policing Officers Association and discuss this issue with the membership. Resnick agreed to wait on making a decision until the police, via the state community policing organization, was consulted.

On January 16, 1997, the New Jersey Community Policing Officers Association met at Nutley Police Headquarters. Approximately 75 officers were in attendance. Sergeant Rogers brought the issue he and Resnick had discussed to the floor. Interestingly, the membership, without one negative comment, agreed to support whatever it would take to assist in the problem-solving process being proposed for Montclair. The membership also voted to establish a New Jersey Community Policing Team to help develop an action plan designed to create a Neighborhood Oriented Policing Team, comprised of police officers from throughout New Jersey, who would assist local community policing bureaus repair neighborhood homes, clean up streets and lots, and conduct workshops on empowerment and crime prevention.

On January 17, Sergeant Rogers called Resnick with the good news. Resnick was ecstatic and asked Rogers if he could set up another meeting with him and Mr. Patrick Morrisey, of the Housing and Urban Development Organization of Orange, New

Jersey. Morrisey is a well-respected man with a vast amount of experience in working on projects like this.

On January 21, all three men—Resnick, Rogers and Pat Morrisey—met in Nutley and discussed a number of issues related to the proposed project. First, the mission statement was discussed. Morrisey suggested that the wording in the statement make it clear that the police were not "pushing themselves" on the people. He wanted to make sure the police were entering the city by "invitation." Resnick agreed and suggested that the invitation come from local police department community policing units.

After much discussion, Resnick, Rogers and Morrisey drafted a mission statement and a proposal to create a statewide community policing team of police officers representing law enforcement from throughout New Jersey.

New Jersey Community-Policing Association
State Community Policing Team
Mission Statement

The New Jersey Community Policing Team, at the invitation of the host police department, will promote and initiate a Neighborhood Oriented Policing program by visiting urban neighborhoods and in partnership with local police, assist citizens in maintaining safe and secure neighborhoods by: (1) helping residents make minor repairs to their homes, which include the installation of locks, alarms and other crime prevention mechanisms; (2) assist citizens in maintaining a safe environment by cleaning up vacant lots, buildings, etc., and (3) conducting workshops on empowerment and crime prevention with emphasis on creating a lasting police-citizen partnership.

When the mission statement was finalized, the next issue discussed was the strategy they would employ to convince key participants that the project had merit. These key participants included police officials, political leaders, religious leaders, the business community and citizens.

Rogers suggested that the outline of a proposed strategy contain common factors shared by all cities and towns. He wanted the outline to be submitted to each host police department for review (in this case Montclair Police would review the project). They, in turn, could use this as a guide in establishing a local strategy which would fit local needs.

Strategy and Guidelines

The Following Responsibilities were Created as a Guideline for this Project:

The New Jersey Community Policing Team is responsible for:

- Selecting a city or township (Montclair was selected in March of 1997);
- Contacting the local police chief/community policing unit and discuss proposal, mission and strategy;
- Submit planning and operational guidelines to local police agency;
- Recruiting police personnel from throughout the state to assist local police;
- Act as troubleshooter in planning and operations.

The local police department is responsible for:

- Developing and planning an operational strategy to suit the needs of their community;
- Contacting key city residents, business people and leaders for assistance;
- Establish priority list of needs;
- Select targets for community action;
- Make assignments; establish a command post.

Why Montclair Was Selected

During the January 21, 1997 meeting between Rogers, Resnick and Morrisey, they discussed a number of cities as possible candidates for the pilot project. From a list of twelve cities originally recommended, they agreed on two as possible prospects.

After further discussion, they reached agreement on a city which, in their collective opinion, had an excellent reputation for its police department, community services and political establishment — Montclair, New Jersey.

On January 27, Montclair Police Chief Thomas Russo was contacted by Rogers and both men discussed the scope and concept of the project. Russo commanded a police department with a reputation of bringing the police and the people together. His commitment to community policing was known statewide.

On January 28, Russo embraced the project and directed Montclair Police Captain Errol Brudner, Supervisor of the Montclair Community Policing Unit, to meet with Rogers and Resnick. Brudner convened a meeting at Montclair Police Headquarters with his entire community policing bureau: Sergeant Roger Terry, Sergeant Kurt Reinhardt and Officer Chuck Lavery. After much discussion, Captain Brudner embraced the idea and received Chief Russo's approval to proceed. Operational and Strategy guidelines were established as follows:

• The Montclair Community Policing Bureau established a leadership team of police personnel and city residents. This team met together and identified community needs to be addressed and the specific neighborhoods the team would be invited to visit.

• Montclair Community Policing Officers were assigned to visit specific neighborhoods in the city and asked residents about their public safety concerns, conducted home security surveys, and noted empty homes and lots filled with debris.

After reviewing the findings of police officers on the street, the leadership team selected specific neighborhoods as the sites the community policing team would visit.

Captain Brudner and his staff met with city officials and explained the details of the project. Within days, the Montclair Fire Department, Public Works Department, City Manager and other key city personnel joined the effort. In addition, the Captain assigned officers to meet with leaders representing business and industry and obtained funding and logistical support. Small businesses, the Salvation Army, the United Way, the clergy and others joined the effort.

The New Jersey Community Policing Team established contacts with two major banks and coordinated press activity, as well as enlisted the support of over 50 police officers from urban and suburban communities throughout New Jersey.

On February 25, a meeting at Montclair Police Headquarters was held with all the participants involved. The planning strategy was refined and finalized by the group. Two new elements were added to the project.

First, Rev. Harold Woods, a local pastor, has a congregation in the middle of one of the streets targeted for a visit by the team. He joined the effort and played a major role in developing communications between the police and the citizens who were going to be affected by this project. Rev. Woods added a spiritual dimension to the project which was applauded by all participants.

The second element added was suggested by East Orange Police Sergeant Frank Cocci. He suggested that teenagers who are involved in the PAL and Explorers be invited to participate. The committee approved of this suggestion and collectively enlisted the assistance of over 100 teenagers from urban and suburban schools. After putting the final touches on the planning and operational issues, the group set April 26, 1997, 8:00 a.m., as the date and time for Project Unity to commence.

Between February and April, project leaders worked night and day to ensure all aspects of the event would be covered. The following agenda was used by project leaders on April 26, 1997.

Project Unity Agenda

- 7:30 a.m./Police personnel, students and participants from outside Montclair arrive at the Bright Hope Baptist Church.

- 8:00 a.m./Rev. Harold Woods welcomes the participants (approximately 200) and prays for a successful day. Montclair Police Chief Thomas Russo welcomes everyone and asks Sergeant Roger Terry to explain the operational plan to all participants.

- 8:30 a.m./Participants leave the church and report to a Command Post established between New and Mission Streets — the target area.

- 8:45 a.m./All personnel are given their assignments and started cleaning up the streets. City workers and police officers knocked down crack houses and made minor home repairs for residents living in the neighborhoods. Middle school students, ages 13-16, cleaned up debris, bottles, vials of drugs, used syringes, weeds and tires from lots and ball fields.

- 12:00 noon/Lunch is served to all participants near the command post and anti-auto theft devices and crime prevention material is given to residents.

- 1:00 p.m./All personnel met at the church where Rev. Woods prayed in thanks for a successful day. Chief Russo gave all participants certificates of award. The project was concluded.

One unplanned event took place at the end of the day. A gang of youths who usually congregate in the neighborhood arrived late in the day and found that their "hang-out" was gone. The neighborhood was returned to the residents. The gang never returned. Phase two of this project began in May of 1997 when the Montclair Police Community Policing Bureau organized community meetings with residents who live on Mission and New Streets. Neighborhood Watch groups were organized and workshops on empowerment were conducted by the police. Community policing patrols were also established in this area.

CHAPTER 9

POLICE AND THE YOUTH

EDUCATION HAS IN AMERICA'S WHOLE HISTORY BEEN THE MAJOR HOPE
FOR IMPROVING INDIVIDUALS AND SOCIETY.

Gunnar Mydral

In the nineties, the image of the police suffered like at no other time in history as a result of three factors. One, the unjustified criticisms of police on a grand scale after highly publicized criminal cases involving law enforcement were sensationalized nationwide. Two, Hollywood characterized police as an enemy of the public in numerous motion pictures and television programs. Three, the failure of law enforcement to develop public relations campaigns designed to counter bad press and false impressions created by the media and movie producers which caused a rapid evaporation of police-community relations.

The one group of people most affected by the erosion of police-community relations in the nineties was America's youth. This fact was confirmed by a survey taken by a major television network revealing that an overwhelming number of America's youth had a bad image and negative feelings toward the police.

In an effort to address "global" negative images from a local level, the Nutley, New Jersey Police Department developed a Police/School Partnership in their community. Its purpose is to improve police-youth relations by giving the police and the youth of the community an opportunity to see the "human side" of each other. The operational procedures of this program is explained at the end of this chapter.

Before the Police/School Partnership was established, the Nutley Police conducted a survey asking high school students how they felt about the Nutley Police Department. Four hundred and forty-seven males and four hundred and thirty-seven females participated in the survey.

An overwhelming majority of students agreed that the crime rate in Nutley was low and the neighborhoods safe as a direct result of the Nutley Police Department's crime prevention/community policing programs and quick responses to emergencies.

Of 884 students surveyed, over 70% admitted having limited contact (negative and positive) with police. Not one student complained of excessive use of force, police brutality, racism or prejudice exhibited by Nutley police officers. Most students agreed that the Nutley Police treated them fairly. However, complaints about negative police behavior and attitude toward young people continued to prevail throughout the school year. Nutley Police officials identified this complaint as legitimate but not widespread. Only a small number of officers with communication problems projected the negative image observed by the youths. Also, nearly 70% of the students expressed a belief that the police had a negative image of them. These figures reflect similar results of a survey taken several years ago in Minnesota.

Armed with the survey results which helped police identify areas they needed to focus on, the Nutley Police created the Police/School Partnership Program in the Nutley Franklin Middle School.

The reason for selecting a middle school for this program was because the students had been exposed to a police officer on a positive basis by participating in the DARE program in elementary school and they were still at an impressionable age. Continuity in positive contact with the police was important to the success of this program.

Police School Partnership
Goals and Objectives

- Increasing student awareness and respect for the legal process and law enforcement.
- Demonstrating the role of police officers in the community.
- Presenting a realistic image of police officers, including the "human component."

- Helping students develop an understanding of the concept of justice.
- Opening lines of communication between the police and the students.
- Presenting a positive image of the police profession.
- Promote awareness and respect for diverse cultures in the community.
- Create and promote violence reduction and conflict resolution methodologies between the police and the students.

Parents, teachers, police officers, the board of education, businessmen, churches and civic groups participate in this program. Its impact transcends from the classroom into the community.

Operational Guidelines

The community policing officer and school officials schedule approximately five classes a week in the middle school. The officer initiates a discussion with the students on a topic of their choice. The setting is informal. Discussions are lively and very informative. After the classroom discussion, the officer has lunch with the students. At the end of the school day, students and officers who see each other on the street initiate positive dialogue with each other. This serves to strengthen police-youth relations.

The positive relationship between the police and students has created a trust and confidence in each other which has impacted juvenile attitude and behavior toward the police for the better. Franklin Middle School administrators, staff and teachers fully support and participate in the partnership. Teachers assisted in organizing an after-school club which has over 150 student members. Club activities include trips to the police academy, law enforcement week activities, courts and other justice department functions. Research projects and numerous sports and educational competitions with police, teachers and students are also organized.

The key to this partnership's success is team work. The Nutley Franklin Middle School under the direction and leadership of the Principal, Dr. James Vivinetto, Vice Principal Ed Fraser and

Teacher John Schwarz and Nutley Police Department officials have created a model for other law enforcement agencies and schools to follow.

Survey Results

The following results reflect the answers Nutley, New Jersey students gave when participating in the survey mentioned on page 42.

1.   **How would you rate the Nutley Police Department? Consider police response time to incidents, crime rate, police-youth relations, police attitude toward the youth.**

Rating	Male Response	Female Response
Poor	10.5%	6.1%
Fair	38.2%	45.5%
Good	45.6%	45.9%
Excellent	5.5%	2.0%

2.   **What factor most influenced your rating as answered in question one?**

Poor:	Negative contact with police, poor police attitude toward youth.
Fair:	Various forms of both negative and positive publicity.
Good:	Police performance, police visibility, low crime rate.
Excellent:	Positive contact with police, and all factors enumerated in the "good" category.

3. Do you have any specific complaints about the police?

Male:	51.4% yes	48.5% no
Female:	48.5% yes	49.1% no

Complaints about police specifically focused on police attitude and behavior when interacting with youth. A large number of youth described some cops as being "mean and rude."

4. How do you think the police feel about you?

Police do not like youth:	Male: 67.7%	Female: 71.3%
Police like youth:	Male: 28.6%	Female: 32.2%

5. Have you ever had contact with a police officer?

Positive:	30.4% male	36.6% female
Negative:	20.5% male	29.2% female
Both:	16.6% male	9.8% female

6. Are you afraid of the police?

Yes	24.0% male	22.4% female
No	75.8% male	77.5% female

CHAPTER 10

CITIZEN SURVEY

WHEN WE FAIL TO SPEAK UP AND SPEAK OUT WE STRIKE A BLOW
AGAINST FREEDOM AND DECENCY AND JUSTICE.

Robert F. Kennedy

Recently, a few police departments have begun to reach out to the public by seeking their opinion about law enforcement "globally" and locally. The Nutley Police Department and Wallington Police Department in New Jersey, circulated a nine-question citizen survey to residents of their respective communities. The surveys were placed in stores, supermarkets, gas stations, public buildings and randomly given to people on the streets. Citizens were encouraged to complete the survey and mail it to police headquarters. Nutley and Wallington received close to 1,000 responses.

Citizens were asked to circle one of four responses — Excellent, Good, Fair, Poor — to the following questions:

1. How do you rate your local police department?
2. How do you rate the appearance of officers on the street?
3. How do you rate the behavior/attitude of police officers?
4. How do you think police view the public?
5. Have you ever been victimized by a crime?
6. If the answer to question 5 is *Yes*, were you treated fairly?
7. When was the last time a police officer said hello to you?
8. If you ever had occasion to call the police, how was the person answering the phone?
9. Would you like to see foot patrols in your community?

Once the results were tabulated by a local resident, they were analyzed by the Community Policing Unit and Police Chief. Where police were able to identify internal and external problems brought to their attention via the survey, action was taken.

CHAPTER 11

CULTURAL DIVERSITY

IT IS NEVER TOO LATE TO GIVE UP YOUR PREJUDICES.

Henry David Thoreau

A hate crime is a criminal act committed upon a person because of his/her race, color, creed or sexual orientation. Hate crimes are committed primarily by juveniles with no other motive than to spread fear throughout a community. When a hate crime occurs in a community, the crime resonates beyond the immediate victim into the community at large.

Nationally, collecting data on hate crimes was ignored until 1988. During that year many states added bias crime data to their Uniform Crime Reports.

Anyone can be victimized by a hate crime. Victimization of bias-related incidents go beyond the obvious immediate damage it causes. Hate crimes create a wounded psyche which must be addressed as soon as possible.

Bias crime victims should be treated with the seriousness that the situation calls for. It is imperative that community policing officers keep their eyes and ears open when interacting with the people in the community they serve. Police officers "on the beat" are in a position to learn much about the people who live and work in the community. This knowledge can be used by officers to proactively address bias in the community.

One effective way to combat hate crime is to educate people, especially youngsters. Police agencies throughout America are training police officers to address the problem of bias crime by introducing cultural diversity programs designed to educate young people at an early age about the impact prejudices have on individual victims and society as a whole.

There are many programs being utilized by the police which highlight the positive characteristics of diverse cultures and emphasize achievements accomplished by people of all ethnic and religious backgrounds. These programs are locally created by police community relations bureaus in partnership with civic and religious organizations.

In addition to school-based programs conducted by police-community relations units, the police themselves have developed sensitivity training programs to help them understand the impact their actions have on minority groups.

Operation A.I.M.
(Awareness-Involvement-Motivation)

Operation A.I.M. underscores the need for students to identify causes of bias-motivated violence and the covert and overt forms of prejudice by heightening their Awareness of the problems many minorities face; by encouraging their Involvement and explaining their importance in prejudice reduction programs; and by Motivating them to become involved in eliminating bias through education and law enforcement.

The standard operating procedure to this program is very cost-effective in that a community policing officer visits students in the elementary and middle schools and shares with them a brief lesson on diverse cultures in the community, accenting the positive contributions made by these individuals.

The officer's presentation lasts approximately 20 minutes. Days and weeks after the officer's classroom discussion, teachers re-enforce the lesson by integrating cultural diversity with routine class lessons.

The purpose of having a community policing officer lead the discussion with students is to emphasize the legal aspects of laws regarding bias crimes and the important role both the students and the police play in preventing hate crimes.

Taking the Initiative

In 1996, an African-American woman was looking for an apartment in Nutley, New Jersey with no success. She wrote a letter to the editor of a local newspaper explaining that her efforts to find a place to live for herself and her 12-year-old daughter was fruitless. She felt she was denied several apartments because of her race.

After Nutley Police Chief Robert DeLitta read the published letter, he assigned his community policing supervisor to look into the matter. Within one week, the police found the women an apartment and furthermore met with real estate managers and apartment owners throughout the township reminding them about laws prohibiting discrimination.

This proactive approach and decisive action by the police brought much praise to the Nutley Police Department by other law enforcement agencies, civil rights groups, and human relations organizations. It showed that when the police and the community work together, bias incidents, whether real or perceived, can be prevented.

CHAPTER 12

POLICE-COMMUNITY PARTNERSHIPS

PEOPLE ARE NOT AN INTERRUPTION OF OUR BUSINESS. PEOPLE ARE OUR
BUSINESS.   *Walter E. Washington*

A successful Police-Community Relations Unit is constantly taking the initiative to create partnerships with the public to maintain a high degree of credibility in the community. Many police agencies have successfully organized police-community partnerships to accomplish their goals and objectives. Below are a few police-community partnerships which can be modeled to meet the needs of any community.

- **Police-Business Alliance:** This partnership is comprised of local business leaders, retailers and community policing officers who meet once every two months to discuss the community's economic and public safety needs.

- **Police-School Partnership:** The Police-School Partnership is described in detail in chapter 8. Classroom activity can be expanded to an after school program by organizing a Police/ Student Partnership Club. Club activities include: trips to police week activities, the police academy, poster contests, trips to the local police station and courts.

- **Police-Clergy Alliance:** This partnership consists of community policing officers and local clergy leaders representing various religious organizations in the community. Once every quarter these individuals meet to discuss issues related to domestic violence, family, homelessness and other issues impacting the community.

- **Crisis Management Team:** This team is comprised of community residents who function under the guidance of the police community relations bureau. The purpose of this team is to defuse any potentially explosive issue which impacts the community. For example, a number of communities have created teams of neighborhood residents representing diverse cultures. In the event a racial incident occurs or racial problems involving the police surface, the Crisis Management Team would be activated to mediate disputes between opposing forces in an effort to defuse potential confrontations.

• **Family Referral Group:** This group is comprised of local family members who have suffered the affects of a child or relative being addicted to drugs. This group is a big asset to police when a parent or drug addicted teen or other relative is seeking guidance or help. Members of this group work with victims and family members through the criminal justice process.

• **Ask The Chief Cable TV Program:** Police agencies are utilizing public access stations on their cable networks. Programs on crime prevention, community policing and other topics including live broadcasts giving the public an opportunity to call in questions directly to the Police Chief have been broadcasted in New Jersey communities.

• **Neighborhood Watch:** Neighborhood watch is a great way to get people involved in addressing community public safety needs through crime prevention. Up-to-date information about neighborhood watch can be obtained from the National Crime Prevention Council. Many communities hold block parties, local neighborhood watch meetings, and town wide meetings to keep members abreast of public safety needs.

• **Apartment Watch:** Similar to Neighborhood Watch, community policing officers meet periodically with apartment managers, owners and superintendents.

• **Community-Police Partnership:** This partnership is comprised of citizens who are genuinely interested in helping formulate community policing methodologies in their community. Citizens who volunteer their time and talent to this group research community policing programs from other areas of the nation, review their value and weigh the possibility of implementing a similar program in their community.

- **Morning Press and Citizens Briefing:** Numerous police departments hold monthly public briefings on the prior months public safety issues. The briefing is usually held at the municipal public library.

CHAPTER 13

INTELLIGENCE GATHERING AND COMMUNITY POLICING

"INTELLIGENCE" IN POLICE WORK IS VERY IMPORTANT IN THE
PREVENTION OF CRIME. KNOWING THE WHO, WHAT, WHEN AND WHERE
OF THE COMMUNITY WE SERVE IS AN IMPORTANT FUNCTION OF
COMMUNITY POLICING.   *Sergeant Steven Rogers*

Violence in America is on the rise and as a result traditional family
structures are shaking at their very foundations. What were once
neighborhoods filled with loving and caring people are becoming
empty streets of sorrow, pain and hopelessness. The United States
is finding itself in the midst of a national catastrophe which is
amounting to the total disintegration of our communities.

A recent national law enforcement publication revealed that at the
end of the last decade three of every five murder victims were
either related to or acquainted with their assailants. Thirty percent
of all female murder victims were slain in domestic violence inci-
dents, and the number of domestic violence incidents in many com-
munities increased by over thirty percent. What is more troubling
is the number of children victimized by crime, especially family
violence.

Law enforcement statistics revealed that approximately 5,000
children under the age of 18 were slain in one year alone. Most of
them were killed during family disputes. In one city it was reported
that, in one year, nine infants under the age of one were shot to
death, while twelve of the same age group were stabbed to death.
Another eight children were burned to death and 235 beaten to
death. Nearly 1,000 children from ages 15-19 died of gunshot
wounds in America during the latter part of the 1980s. As we
approach the 21st century, family violence and street violence are
increasing with teen suicide and hate crimes.

As of the mid-nineties, skinhead gangs have been reported to be in at least 100 cities across the USA recruiting more than 3,000 gang members in 37 states. More than 350 white supremacists groups are operating in America.

In 1996 and 1997, militia groups have increased their activity by using terrorist acts against the government. The 1996 Oklahoma City bombing and the 1997 incidents involving the Republic of Texas militia should serve as a warning to all of us as to what is yet to come if we do not awaken to the fact that information, no matter how small it may be, is an important law enforcement tool.

Community policing officers are in the unique position to address potential criminal activity by gathering intelligence information from the very people who they interact with on a daily basis. Who better than the community policing officer knows the who, what, when, where and why of the people who live and work in the neighborhoods they patrol.

Community policing officers are in a position to make important observations in the neighborhoods they patrol and detect elements which have the potential of becoming law enforcement problems.

For example, in one New Jersey township, a community policing officer walking his beat went to use a public telephone on a street corner. As he was dialing a phone number he noticed a number of Nazi Swastikas carved in the glass of the telephone booth. During the next few days, he began to ask questions about the bias graffiti and learned that a skinhead gang leader moved into the area to recruit teens to join his gang. A potential gang problem was prevented by quick action on the part of the police and community leaders.

In another city, community policing officers learned of a man who lost his job, was out of money and began to fight with his wife and kids often enough for neighbors to become concerned. The officers visited the man and found that the family situation was in a state of despair. It was apparent to the police that, if some help wasn't found for this family soon, a major domestic violence problem would occur.

Community policing officers contacted a family crisis worker and local member of the clergy who assisted the family. A domestic violence incident was prevented and a family was no doubt saved from collapse.

In other communities, citizens have provided police with information about drug dealers, crack houses, and other criminal activity resulting in arrests, prosecutions and convictions of criminal suspects. These citizens have gained a genuine trust for the police who are walking in their neighborhoods.

CHAPTER 14

VICTIM ORIENTED POLICING

IN THE 1990S PEOPLE ARE NOT ONLY VICTIMIZED BY CRIMINALS, THEY
ARE ALSO VICTIMIZED BY AN INSENSITIVE CRIMINAL JUSTICE SYSTEM.

A New Jersey crime victim

Victim Oriented Policing is a policing methodology designed to address the needs of crime victims during immediate and initial contact they have with the criminal justice system via the local police by minimizing the trauma crime victims suffer by initiating a more responsible and sensitive approach during initial contact between the police and the victim. VOP also encourages crime victims to seek long term solutions to the problems they are facing through conflict management. VOP enables police to utilize local resources for the purpose of initiating a process which leads to the identification of root causes and long term solutions to specific crimes such as those related to family violence and bias incidents.

The police and the community establish a resource umbrella involving public and private social service organizations, mental health services, family counseling services, religious organizations and educational services in an effort to assist crime victims through Victim Oriented Policing.

Many police agencies can secure small grants in the amount of $2,000 or more from their county victim witness coordinators for the purpose of enhancing victim oriented policing strategies.

CHAPTER 15

VOLUNTEERS

THE PATRIOT VOLUNTEER, HELPING TO KEEP THE PEACE IN HIS
COMMUNITY, IS THE MOST RELIABLE "POLICE OFFICER" IN THE NATION.
Sergeant Steven Rogers

Volunteers can play a major role in enhancing local community policing organizations. It is recommended that community policing officers seek to recruit volunteers by utilizing the following resources:

* Local newspaper releases or ads;
* Community policing officers visiting local service organizations, PTAs, senior citizens groups;
* Calling colleges for interns;
* Calling the local high school for volunteer student help.

In addition to the above, many police agencies have police auxiliary officers who dedicate much time to assisting their police department. The possibility of deploying these officers on foot patrol should be explored.

Auxiliary officers could serve as the extended eyes and ears of the regular police force. They could help build bridges between the police and the community by their visibility in neighborhoods where petty crimes, drug trafficking and other criminal activity is running rampant.

Auxiliary officers can help establish important community contacts for the regular police and encourage citizen participation in police-community partnerships. These volunteers can be a vital resource for police agencies in combating crime and promoting positive police community relations well into the next century.

CHAPTER 16

COMMUNITY CONFLICTS

In November, 1997, the Nutley, New Jersey Police Department community policing efforts paid big dividends in an area of the community where an explosive situation was developing. The following report described the problems which surfaced in one neighborhood and what the police did to address community needs.

Introduction
Nutley NJ Police Dept Community-Police Partnership Report

Business owners in the area of Bloomfield Avenue and High Street have been suffering economically as a result of the lack of parking in that particular area. This problem has escalated into a situation which requires police intervention in both enforcement of existing laws and mediation of disputing parties. Specifically, the target area being addressed is High Street (the north and south side) between Funston Place and Bloomfield Avenue.

On the north side of High Street exists a dentist office, hair dresser, tailor and seat cover business. On the south side exists a deli, vacuum cleaner repair shop and another small business. In front of the businesses on the north side of High Street exist five meters; in front of the businesses on the south side there is no parking.

As a result of the escalating problems in this area, business owners requested the intervention of the Nutley Community Policing Unit. Hence, the Community Relations Unit Community-Police Partnership under the Chairmanship of Mr. Walt Smith convened a meeting with all interested parties on October 23, 1997, 7:30 p.m. at the Nutley Police Department for purposes of utilizing a problem oriented policing methodology which includes the community in: (a) mediation of disputed parties; and (b) seeking a solution agreeable to all parties.

Problem-Summarized

The cause for the existing problem is that the hair dresser has a high volume of business which requires customers to park on a long term basis in the target area; in addition the smaller businesses require very short-term parking for the high volume of customers they service.

The Community-Police Partnership has found that businesses requiring long-term parking have customers who park at the meters for several hours, thus impacting the businesses requiring only short-term parking. In addition, three other problems exist: (1) police enforcement of existing parking laws has been inconsistent; (2) meters reflect a three-hour parking limit whereas a sign reflects a one-hour parking limit, adding to the confusion; (3) dozens of vehicles from individuals employed at Hoffman LaRoche park in the only available parking spaces left on High Street for up to eight hours with little or no enforcement by police.

Recommendations

The Community-Police Partnership believes that a solution serving the best interest of the businesses and residents in the area is attainable with the cooperation of both law enforcement and other government agencies in the township. It is very clear that the impact that existing conditions is having on the businesses in the area is not good for the community and the businesses in the target area.

After two hours of discussing this issue with all interested parties, a number of solutions were agreed upon. Hence, the Community-Police Partnership requests that the following recommendations be reviewed by the Chief of Police and forwarded to the appropriate authorities for further action.

1. We recommend that the five meters be removed from the area of High Street and Bloomfield Ave. and replaced with 15- or 30-minute parking signs. JUSTIFICATION: Since meters are not installed for revenue purposes and are installed to insure a reasonable turnover rate for business owners in specific areas of town, a 15- or 30-minute parking ordinance for this area would impact positively on all businesses in the area. The

township will not lose anything by implementing this recommendation and there would be positive economic impact on the businesses.

2. We recommend that approximately 200 feet of Funston Place (North from High Street) become an unlimited parking area. JUSTIFICATION: This area of Funston Place has no houses bordering the street. Hence, no resident would be impacted and businesses requiring long-term parking, i.e., a few hours, would be satisfied.

3. We recommend that in order to ensure that each recommendation serves its intended purpose, the police department should implement directed patrols and park and walks in the targeted area. JUSTIFICATION: Police presence would have positive impact in the area by ensuring that parking regulations are enforced and furthermore create a proactive approach to problem-solving in the area.

Conclusion

The Community-Police Partnership understands that a governmental process is necessary to make some of the changes recommended by this committee. Hence, all parties were advised that what is being proposed may take some time. However, what is important is that all parties were agreeable to these recommendations and, furthermore, have agreed to work together with the police community relations unit to do what is in the best interest of the community as well as all parties concerned.

The process in which this committee has undertaken truly brought to surface the spirit of what community policing and community-police partnerships are all about. It is in this spirit that we forward these recommendations. Each party has been given a copy of this report with a commitment that we will advise them of our progress.

This report was forwarded to Chief Robert DeLitta of the Nutley Police Department who, in turn, forwarded it to other local government authorities for action. In addition, individuals in the neighborhood affected, business owners, and committee participants were given a copy of this report.

CHAPTER 17

THE INFORMATION HIGHWAY AND COMMUNITY POLICING

The Nutley Police Department Community Policing Unit has utilized the Internet to communicate with township residents and youth. Nutley PD@aol.com is the e-mail number residents are using to give police suggestions about the quality of life and public safety of the community.

Since this community policing program was implemented, the Nutley Police Department has received over 20 e-mails a week from residents and youth. The e-mail is read by the supervisor of the community policing unit and the Chief of Police for action within 24 hours.

In addition, the police community relations unit has established an electronic newsletter which is e-mailed to everyone on the Nutley Police e-mail address list. The newsletter contains crime prevention tips, community policing programs and other issues related to public safety and quality of life issues.

CHAPTER 18

COMMUNITY POLICING
The Dawning of a New Day

THE PUNISHMENT OF WISE MEN WHO REFUSE TO TAKE PART IN THE
OFFICES OF GOVERNMENT IS TO LIVE UNDER THE GOVERNMENT OF
UNWISE MEN.
                                                    Plato

Community Policing is a philosophy intended to improve police-community relations by creating a partnership between the people who live and work in the community and the local police. The Community Policing unit is a catalyst for problem-solving in the community.

Community Policing gives the people an opportunity to get to know their police force and to get involved in crime fighting through proactive policing programs. Community Policing will work in any community provided that the entire police agency serving the community becomes involved in the process of meeting the needs of the public.

Many unwise police administrators and patrol officers have dispelled Community Policing as "just another program" designed to appease the public. These traditional bound leaders have failed their officers, communities and profession. In June of 1992, the law enforcement publication, *Fresh Perspectives*, outlined a number of things traditional bound officers and administrators do to undermine Community Policing. These things are:

• Oversell Community Policing as the panacea for every ill that plagues a community;

• Failing to clearly define police service, effectiveness and problem-solving;

• Creating special units to perform Community Policing thus excluding the rest of the department;

- Creating a "soft" image when addressing crime;

- Isolating the community from the police department.

Police administrators, who embrace Community Policing, know full-well it works. Perhaps Los Angeles Police Commissioner Willie Williams says it best: *"Community Policing means more than police presence. It means speaking with people who live and work in the community and find out what's important to them, what they want and try to tailor some police services to meet those demands."*

Neighborhood Leadership Initiative

One method many police agencies have utilized to encourage police-community partnerships is through Neighborhood Leadership Initiatives (NLI).

Community Policing Units encourage citizens to report public safety and quality of life problems in their respective neighborhoods. After the problems are received by the police, the community policing officers return to the neighborhoods where the problems are cited and ask residents for input in problem-solving. NLI creates a feeling of ownership by residents who wish to maintain safe streets in their community.

The sun is setting on traditional bound police executives and police officers who are not embracing change. A new day has dawned for the 21st Century Police Officer. A day which encourages police officers to use their creativity and intelligence in addressing the quality of life and public safety of the community; a day which recognizes Community Policing as the solution to America's crime problems.

CHAPTER QUESTIONS
FOR 21st CENTURY POLICING

Chapter 1

- What problems do leaders in law enforcement face when implementing community policing?
- List some of the problems enumerated in question one and explain what affect they have on (1) the police agency; and (2) the community.
- What is meant by the "tower" when making reference to police leadership?
- Identify and explain one leadership style which hinders community policing?
- Explain the MBWA methodolgy of leadership.

Chapters 2 and 3

- Explain what the term "five percenter" means.
- List a number of ways police agencies could prevent the emergence of "five percenters."
- Explain why you think it is difficult for good cops to turn in bad cops.
- What is meant by "local issues having global impact?"
- Name two law enforcement incidents outlined in this book which have had negative "global impact" on law enforcement and explain how these incidents could have been handled differently.

Chapters 4 and 5

- Identify two management failures in law enforcement and explain why these management methodologies will not enhance community policing.
- Explain why educational standards should be elevated in the police recruitment process.
- Name five basic educational requirements which should be included in police candidate training.
- What is meant by "siege mentality?"

Chapters 6 and 7

- What is "Police Mystique?"
- Suggest two ways a police department can remove "mystique" from their organization
- Explain Random Patrol
- Explain Directed Patrol
- Explain what is meant by "tunnel vision."
- What is PWT and how can it be used in YOUR community?
- What is Vertical Patrol? Explain its operation.

Chapter 8

- Define the "broken window" theory of policing.
- Explain the link between QLP and Crime.
- Identify the five-step process used by the Montclair Police Department in implementing Project Unity.
- Briefly explain how YOU would establish a similar project like the one Montclair established, in your community.
- What role do the following organizations have in the community policing concept? (1) Business; (2) Educational; (3) Clergy; (4) Government.

Chapters 9, 10 and 11

- List the goals and objectives of (1) Police/School Partnership Survey; (2) Citizen Survey.
- Create a Citizen Survey and list nine questions you would ask the citizens of your community about the police department.
- What is a hate crime?
- Explain why a program like Operation AIM is an important component of community policing.

Chapter 12

- Review the Police/Community Partnerships listed in this chapter and explain how each of these would or would not be organized in your community and why.

Chapter 13

- What is meant by intelligence gathering?
- How can the community policing officer gather intelligence in the community he works?
- Identify, from this chapter, at least one police action which hurt the image of law enforcement and explain how you would have handled the action differently.

Chapters 14 and 15

- What is VOP?
- What is meant by "resource umbrella?"
- Develop a "resource umbrella" in your community. (List resources.)
- What role can volunteers play in the implementation of community policing?
- Identify where you may find volunteers.

Chapters 16 and 17

- Write a short summary on how you would address a small community conflict in your township.
- Write a short summary on how you can utilize the Internet for community policing purposes.

Chapter 18

- Explain what NLI means and how it works.
- Compare traditional bound policing with your concept of community policing. Identify advantages and disadvantages.

INDEX

Table of Contents

Introduction	Fear	Mental Rehearsal	Off-Duty Survival
The Art of Tactical Thinking	Command Presence	Effects of Sudden Stress	Never Say Die
Awareness	Tactical Terminology	Critique	When It's Over

Please send _____ copy(ies) of *Developing the Survival Attitude* at a cost of $9.95 per copy. I understand that if I am not totally satisfied I may return it (them) within 10 days for a full refund. I have enclosed payment as indicated below, including postage, tax and handling.

Quantity Discounts Available!

PLEASE PRINT CLEARLY   PLEASE PRINT CLEARLY

Name _____

Street Address _____ Apt. No. _____

Town & State _____ Zip Code _____

(___) _____
Daytime Phone Number

Credit Card #: _____
(M.C./Visa/AMEX/Discover)   (Expiration Date)

TOTAL COST OF ITEMS	$ _____
Postage & Handling (*INSURED*) ($4.00 for the first item, plus $3.00 for the second item, and $2.00 for each additional item.)	$ _____
Optional First Class ($2.00 extra per order)	$ _____
Sales Tax _____ %	$ _____
AMOUNT DUE:	$ _____

RETURN THIS FORM WITH YOUR CHECK, PURCHASE ORDER OR VOUCHER TO:

LOOSELEAF LAW PUBLICATIONS, INC.
P.O. Box 650042, Fresh Meadows, N.Y. 11365-0042

Telephone Order by Credit Card (718) 359-5559 *also* **24 Hour Fax No. (718) 539-0941**
http://www.LooseleafLaw.com   e-mail: llawpub@erols.com

A Summary of
U.S. Supreme Court Decisions

These books contain the summary of the opinion actually written by the
Court's Reporter of Decisions.

The accompanying *Windows* software contains the full report
with dissenting and concurring opinions.

For The Criminal Justice Community	For Corrections *Available Fall 1998*
Enhanced! Now over 145 *United States Supreme Court Cases*	*Over 100* *United States Supreme Court Cases*

NEW!

For The Criminal Justice Community

Enhanced! Now over 145
United States Supreme Court Cases

Confessions	Exclusionary Rule
Probable Cause	Identification
Juveniles	Use of Force
Employment Rights	Warrantless Arrests
Stop and Frisk	Search Warrants

For Corrections
Available Fall 1998

Over 100
United States Supreme Court Cases

Prisons/Jails	Juveniles
Parole	Death Penalty
Probation	Sentencing

and much, much more!

These books and software are subdivided according to topic and party name.
Easy-to-use software...look up decisions by party name, topic or conduct single or multiple word searches.
Use the copy and paste feature for report writing.

"A Summary of U.S. Supreme Court Decisions"
Avoid costly liability actions...familiarize yourself with the decisions that have the greatest impact.
Faced with today's legal issues...these books are a *MUST!*

Please send _____ copy(ies) of *A Summary of U.S. Supreme Court Decisions for the Criminal Justice Community* at a cost of **$29.95** per copy. I understand that if I am not totally satisfied I may return it (them) within 10 days for a full refund. I have enclosed payment as indicated below, including postage, tax and handling.

Please send _____ copy(ies) of *A Summary of U.S. Supreme Court Decisions for Corrections** at a cost of **$29.95** per copy. I understand that if I am not totally satisfied I may return it (them) within 10 days for a full refund. I have enclosed payment as indicated below, including postage, tax and handling.

*Available Fall 1998 - Order Now! Will be shipped as soon as available.

Quantity Discounts Available!

PLEASE PRINT CLEARLY

PLEASE PRINT CLEARLY

Name _____

Street Address _____ Apt. No. _____

Town & State _____ Zip Code _____

Daytime Phone Number
( ) _____

Credit Card #: _____
(M.C./Visa/AMEX/Discover) _____ (Expiration Date)

TOTAL COST OF ITEMS $ _____

Postage & Handling (*INSURED*) $ _____
($5.00 for the first item, plus $4.00 for the second item, and $2.00 for each additional item.)

Optional First Class *($2.00 extra per order)* $ _____

Sales Tax _____ % $ _____

AMOUNT DUE: $ _____

RETURN THIS FORM WITH YOUR CHECK, PURCHASE ORDER OR VOUCHER TO:

LOOSELEAF LAW PUBLICATIONS, INC.
P.O. Box 650042, Fresh Meadows, N.Y. 11365-0042
Telephone Order by Credit Card (718) 359-5559 *also* 24 Hour Fax No. (718) **539-0941**
www.LooseleafLaw.com   e-mail: llawpub@erols.com

The *Path* of the *Warrior*

AN ETHICAL GUIDE TO PERSONAL & PROFESSIONAL DEVELOPMENT IN THE FIELD OF CRIMINAL JUSTICE

By Larry F. Jetmore, Ph.D., Captain, Hartford PD, Ret.

Warriors are people who have chosen to walk a separate path, different from others. This book points the way to the path by sharing an ancient philosophy and code of honor used by *King Arthur's Knights of the Round Table, The French Foreign Legion, Navy Seals* and *Green Berets.* This book is written for and about those who have embraced the field of criminal justice as a way of life. It provides an ethical framework leading to personal development, growth, and professional success.

This book is written for police officers and students of law enforcement who are searching for practical ways to resolve the complicated ethical dilemmas faced by those who wear a badge and carry a gun.

People who have chosen policing as a way of life are especially vulnerable to a slow draining of enthusiasm and positive energy. In giving so much of themselves to others, over time it becomes increasingly difficult to rekindle the fire that first drew them to policing. This book offers a different way of thinking and living -- provides intervention techniques -- that many have found helpful in guarding their inner spirits while going where others fear to tread.

Answering the question, How does today's officer determine the 'right' thing to do? is the primary focus of this work. We will explore different paths to taking positive control of our lives and stimulating personal and professional growth.

Please send _____ copy(ies) of *The Path of the Warrior* at a cost of **$19.95** per copy. I understand that if I am not totally satisfied I may return it (them) within 10 days for a full refund. I have enclosed payment as indicated below, including postage, tax and handling.

Quantity Discounts Available!

PLEASE PRINT CLEARLY   PLEASE PRINT CLEARLY

TOTAL COST OF ITEMS	$ _____
Postage & Handling (*INSURED*) (*$5.00 for the first item, plus $4.00 for the second item, and $2.00 for each additional item.*)	$ _____
Optional First Class (*$2.00 extra per order*)	$ _____
Sales Tax _____ %	$ _____
AMOUNT DUE:	$ _____

Name _____

Street Address _____ Apt. No. _____

Town & State _____ Zip Code _____

(___) _____
Daytime Phone Number

Credit Card #: _____
(M.C./Visa/AMEX/Discover)

_____
(Expiration Date)

RETURN THIS FORM WITH YOUR CHECK, PURCHASE ORDER OR VOUCHER TO:

LOOSELEAF LAW PUBLICATIONS, INC.

P.O. Box 650042, Fresh Meadows, N.Y. 11365-0042

Telephone Order by Credit Card **(718) 359-5559** *also* 24 Hour Fax No. **(718) 539-0941**

www.LooseleafLaw.com   e-mail: llawpub@erols.com

The Only Police Promotion Books of Their Kind!

HOW TO BE SUCCESSFUL ON PROMOTION EXAMINATIONS INVOLVING *WRITTEN* ASSESSMENT EXERCISES	HOW TO BE SUCCESSFUL ON PROMOTION EXAMINATIONS INVOLVING *ORAL* ASSESSMENT EXERCISES

By: Donald J. Schroeder Ph.D., Commanding Officer, 81st Pct. N.Y.C.P.D., Ret. and Frank A. Lombardo, Deputy Inspector, N.Y.C.P.D., Ret.

Dealing With Assessment Exercises such as:

''*In Basket,*'' ''*Orals*'' and ''*Videos*''

Now you can prepare for assessment exams.

Believe it!

PROMOTION SERIES

(CIRCLE prices of items desired)

Oral Assessment Exercises for Police **24.95**
Written Assessment Exercises for Police **24.95**
*Supervision Card Course 17.95
  *Supervision Card Course *Windows* program 19.95
The New Dictionary of Legal Terms 10.95
Civil Service Question Set *(6 Books, postage = 5.00)* ... 24.95
          Supervision - Administration - Personnel Management
Police Operations - Reading Comprehension - Communications
          ($4.95 per single copy, circle title(s))
Emergency Responder's Pocket Field Guide 5.95

(CIRCLE prices of items desired)

A Summary of US Supreme Court Decisions for the
  Criminal Justice Community *(Book and Software)* $29.95
NEW! Community Policing - A Guide for POs & Citizens 10.95
The "HOW" of Criminal Law . . . *(P&H $3.00)* 7.95
Management Quizzer . . . . *(P&H $3.00)* 6.95
Pistol Instruction Handbook. . . . *(P&H $3.00)* 7.95
Police Officer's Response Guide 29.95
Police Promotion Manual 16.95
*Police Supervisor's Test Manual $24.95
*Police Supervisor's Test Manual *Windows* program 19.95

TOTAL COST OF ITEMS	$
Postage & Handling *(INSURED)*	$
($5.00 for the first item, plus $4.00 for the second item, and $2.00 for each additional item, unless otherwise indicated.)	
Optional First Class *($2.00 extra per order)*	$
Sales Tax ___ %	$
AMOUNT DUE:	$

Name _____

Street Address _____ Apt. No. _____

Town & State _____ Zip Code _____

(___) _____
Daytime Phone Number

Credit Card #: _____
          (M.C./Visa/AMEX/Discover)

_____
(Expiration Date)

RETURN THIS FORM WITH YOUR CHECK, PURCHASE ORDER OR VOUCHER TO:

LOOSELEAF LAW PUBLICATIONS, INC.

P.O. Box 650042, Fresh Meadows, N.Y. 11365-0042

Telephone Order by Credit Card (718) 359-5559 *also* **24 Hour Fax No. (718) 539-0941**

www.LooseleafLaw.com   e-mail: llawpub@erols.com